It Shouldn'

CW01647363

to a PhD Student

How to thrive, not just survive, during your PhD

Professor Elaine Cloutman-Green

The Girlymicrobiologist

Copyright © 2025 Professor Elaine Cloutman-Green BEM

All rights reserved.

ISBN: 978-1-80605-075-8

DEDICATION

To my sister Claire, this book contains the advice that I know you would have passed on to me during the dark times of my PhD. I hope the advice contained within can be the light for others who need it to find a way forward and help your memory live on.

CONTENTS

ACKNOWLEDGMENTS

To all my PhD students, past, present and future. I've learnt as much from you as I hope you've learnt from me, thank you for letting me share your journey.

To my family and friends, who put up with me during my PhD journey, especially Mr and Mummy Girlymicro. You were there through all the pain, as well as all the joy. I'll never be able to truly repay you. To my dad, Dr Girlymicro, you showed me that this was possible. Thank you.

Thank you to everyone who read drafts, commented and contributed to this book. Science takes a village, and it turns out that book writing is no different. A special thank you to Alice Wallace for helping design the book cover and to Jon Cloutman-Green for his photography skills.

Finally, thank you to Dr Sam Watkins and Dr Helen Rickard, two of the most wonderful PhD students you could hope for. Thank you both for agreeing to contribute your experiences as part of this book. You have both made me a better scientist and supervisor by working with you.

FOREWORD

No matter who you are, or how well prepared you are, a PhD is a tough project. There will always be challenging times and days when it feels impossible, but not every day needs to be that way, and the journey as a whole should be one you look back on fondly. This book aims to help you prepare for what a PhD actually is, find the joy in academic exploration, and give you the tools you need to not only help you navigate the PhD, but to thrive both during and after completion.

As a scientist with over 2 decades of experience, who has sat on both sides of the viva table, and with multiple successful PhD students, I thought it would be useful to capture the lessons I've learnt, and the advice that I now give to my students, those I mentor, and anyone who reaches out for advice and help. Thus, this book was born.

The content of this book is based on the Girlymicrobiologist blog: https://girlymicrobiologist.com/, which posts weekly linked to all things science, Infection Prevention and Control, and leadership. Although I come from a life sciences background and will use both that and my microbiology discipline as examples, the lessons linked to how to get onto a PhD programme and manage the challenges whilst you are on one should apply to any academic setting.

To help you navigate, this book is structured into three sections, what to think about before you are on a PhD programme, information to help you whilst you are on one, and finally, how to use your time on a PhD to prepare for your future. Section two is split into a structure based on a standard 3-year UK based PhD, but it can be altered to apply to a part time or other PhD setting. The structure is just meant to give you information based on how far through the PhD project you are, in order to help you think about what might be useful at the beginning, the middle and towards the end. There are also activities available to support several of the chapters on the https://girlymicrobiologist.com website, just head over to the books page.

Undertaking a PhD is one of the few times in your academic life that you truly have the freedom to try things out without fear, to fully embrace academic curiosity to go down rabbit holes that may not immediately pay off and are not fully constrained by someone else's grant schedule or reporting structure. It is a time to work out who you are, both as a person and an academic, and to develop skills that will pay off for the rest of your career and life. It should be a time that you look back on fondly, and where there are days when you shout 'yes' when something finally clicks, or an experiment finally works. This book is written in the hope that it will help you find more good days than bad, and that you can use those days to achieve all you can to prepare for a glorious future. Good luck and let me know when you pass that viva.

SECTION ONE – HOW TO GET ONTO A PHD PROGRAMME

CHAPTER ONE: KNOWING YOUR WHY

So, you've decided to do a PhD…

Studying for a PhD should be one of the best times of your life, and an experience that will stay with you forever. Taking on such a big project can sometimes feel overwhelming, and this book aims to help you break down all the stages, from application to completion, into manageable pieces to help you make the right decisions for you, and to aid in managing some of the complexity integral to the process. A PhD can, with the right support, be a joyful experience but more than that it can change your life. I hope this book gives you the confidence to dive in and make the right decisions on how to undertake a PhD in a way that works for you and your circumstances.

Often people think that the main step to getting onto a PhD is deciding that you want to and then overcoming the barriers to get onto a course. They think the main work begins once they've gotten onto a programme. The truth is pretty different, however. The main work actually begins with understanding your why. Why is a PhD the next step? Why now? Why would it help you? Why this subject? Why this place? Why deep down do you want it?

PhD's, no matter how committed and excited you are to start one, are hard. They are challenging projects that run over years, and so your motivation and momentum also need to last over the same period. The initial excitement of succeeding in getting onto a programme will last you months but is very unlikely to get you over the finish line. To maintain commitment over a time frame of years you need to be driven by much more than getting the letters Dr in front of your name, no matter how lovely that is. Over the last decade I've spent time talking with a lot of people who come to me saying they want a PhD and my first question is always why? I ask this not just because it is the question you will always get asked in your PhD interviews, but because your answer will determine several things. The first of which is letting me know is how much thinking have you've done, and how much investigation into the nitty gritty of a PhD that you have already undertaken.

Starting a discussion with someone where I ask why they've decided to do a PhD is a good way to check how much thinking has been done about:

a) what a PhD actually is?
b) how will it enable to them achieve their aspirations?

A PhD is not the end game after all, it's a step on a pathway.

Now, if you are an undergraduate, you may be focussed on a PhD as the next educational step. In this case you may not yet have clarity about where it will lead, it's more about keeping your options open and exploring further career choices. However, for someone who's already working and wants to progress their career, this question holds a lot more weight as you are likely to be more resource limited (in terms of time) and probably need higher levels of clarity prior to committing. The same is true if you are looking at using the opportunity to change direction or achieve a new focus on an alternative path.

The way someone answers the 'why' question helps me gauge how far along the thought process someone is. When I ask this question in an interview, it also helps me gauge how committed someone is, as it shows me if they have invested the time to really think about their why and how it serves their purpose and values.

To start thinking about how to answer this question, it is helpful to undertake some self-reflection, starting with:

- Where have I come from?
- Where am I now?
- What am I hoping to achieve?

Where you have come from is important as it will help determine not only your readiness, but some of your access to support in the application process, alongside what you might want to highlight in admission paperwork. Not everyone applying needs to have a masters degree. Not everyone who applies for a PhD needs to know someone who already has one. Knowing where your current experience and access to networks lies however, helps you determine where you might need to take additional steps in order to increase your chances of application success. Hopefully this book will give you a good head start along the way, no matter your starting point, however.

Where you are now is a crucial piece of thinking to about how you will undertake a PhD. This thinking should include everything from where you are living and if you'd be willing to travel or relocate, to what matters most to you in terms of your personal and work life. Do you have, or are you anticipating, having caring commitments? What do you value in terms of your work life balance? This can include everything from the fact that your Saturday night out with your girlfriends as a re-set, to having unwind time on your own with a good book or baking to relax. Everyone is different, and everyone's needs are different. You don't have to justify what those needs are, but you should be aware of them so that you make sure that your ongoing decision making takes these core needs and values into account, as you will never be happy if you make decisions that cause you to misalign with these core requirements.

Where you hope to end up will have a massive impact on which PhD is right for you. There will be no point in doing a professional doctorate if your eventual aim is to become a clinical academic. If your aim is to end up in industry, then you may want to choose a PhD that is closely linked into an industrial partnership. Not everyone who wants to do a PhD is doing so because they want to end up in an academic career. There are all kinds of reasons why someone decides to undertake such a big project. Doing the thinking to understand what your big dreams are, even if you never want to voice them to someone else because they feel unachievable, is important as a PhD should be a step towards you delivering on those aspirations.

This then leads onto some more specific questions:

- What type of PhD?
- What subject of PhD?
- Where do you see a PhD taking you to in 15 years time?
- Why now?

Being able to answer these questions will enable you to take the next steps in thinking what PhD may be right for you. There are no right and wrong answers, only ones that mean you will find something that allows you to get the most out of the experience to come.

CHAPTER TWO: WHAT ARE THE DIFFERENT ROUTES TO A PHD?

Many moons ago, when I was an undergraduate, I only really knew about one type of PhD programme. The type where you signed on for three years of full-time study based in a university, and where you might get a fourth year to write up, as it was rare to complete your viva within the initial three research years. PhD programmes are actually so much more diverse than that, I just didn't realise it when I was starting out. There are so many different options and being aware of these can impact, not just your PhD, but the career path that comes afterwards.

Let's start by talking about the different types of PhD's available. The main type that I am going to talk about in detail throughout this book is a research doctorate, or what is known as a Doctor of Philosophy. There is a reason it holds this name, and that is because the focus of the PhD is linked to developing an approach to thinking and a love of seeking wisdom and pursuing knowledge. If you wish to develop an academic career therefore, a Doctor of Philosophy is the most appropriate qualification to seek in order to act as a foundation and develop academic credibility.

There are other types of doctoral level qualifications available however, depending on your starting point. These often fall into the category of professional doctorates, and are possible to get in many professional disciplines, from Healthcare Science to Engineering or Music. These differ from a research doctorate, in that they include research components alongside advanced studies linked to the professional discipline. This means that they will often have higher levels of taught components that run alongside the research sections. When talking about professional doctorates, this form of PhD can be highly valuable when looking to advance in a professional capacity, but may have some limitations, due to the reduced research component, in developing a purely academic career. Awareness of this option is a reason why understanding where you wish to utilise your doctorate after achieving it is key, when making your initial decisions about which pathway may be most appropriate for you. If you choose your route without knowing your reasons for choosing a specific PhD path, you could close off some future possibilities without truly being aware at the time of the decision.

The route that might work best for you will also depend on personal factors, such as finances, learning preferences and available time. For instance, standard PhD terms vary between countries, with PhD programmes in the USA generally taking much longer, with 4 – 8 years being normal, and PhDs in Sweden and other Scandinavian countries often taking 4 - 5 years. There are also differences between subject areas, with social sciences/humanities PhDs frequently taking 4 – 6 years, compared to the 3 – 4 years I was used to within scientific research. Even the assessments can vary, with some countries allowing you to submit research papers as part of your thesis, and others requiring a separate document developed specifically for the assessment. It is therefore important to know what options are available to you, and make some informed decisions based on your personal circumstances about which types of PhD programme you would be interested in pursuing.

One big consideration, for many of us, are the funding options linked to undertaking a PhD. Funding comes in a wide variety of shapes and forms, and the options are much broader than the university funded ones that I knew about during my undergraduate study. Some of the common ones include:

- Stipend funded
    - Research council funded
    - University
    - Industry funded
- Self-funded, commonly known as unfunded
- In-post training
- Fellowship funded

Thinking about what route to PhD you can choose is important. Some, like fellowships, come with substantial resource in terms of matched salary and both educational and consumables funding, but are highly competitive and will likely take you over a year to prepare. Others are much more under your control, like self-funded, but require you to have resources of your own to begin with.

Stipend funded is the route most people think of when talking about undertaking a PhD. This is where you are awarded a living allowance, similar to a salary, as part of your programme. There are often some differences from a standard salary however, as the funding may be tax free, and it is often paid periodically based on an academic calendar rather than monthly. You may also be entitled to additional tax and other benefits based on your student status, which may not apply to all other routes. For this type of study, you generally apply for a project where the funding and requirements of the PhD have been set out by a supervisor or to a doctoral school that is already established within a university. These contracts are more like fixed term jobs where you deliver on a set of parameters over the course of the contract.

All stipend funded PhDs may be broadly similar, in that they fund some form of living allowance or stipend, they do however differ in a few other details. If a PhD is being advertised as part of a large intake linked to a doctoral school, they are sometimes funded for 4 years instead of 3, and the specific PhD project you are going to be doing is often not confirmed until after you have undertaken all of your year 1 rotations. These rotations will usually let you move between 3 or 4 departments so that you can get to know potential supervisors, undertake mini projects to see how much the topics are of interest to you, and let you engage with peer support. They are often a good choice if you have not had enough experience to feel certain enough to decide on a precise PhD topic, and they provide real exposure to the labs you may be working in to help you make informed decisions. You will not be guaranteed that you will receive your first-choice project however, and the time taken is longer, which means you would usually be expected to have fully submitted your thesis by the end of year 4, rather than having an additional writing up year.

Other stipend funded 4-year PhDs will have the requirement to undertake an MRes, or Master of Research, in their first year. The aim of this is to give you a head start in developing your research skills, in a more structured setting that combines research and taught components. This means that when you start your PhD in year 2 you already have a number of the skills required. This again means you will usually be expected to have completed and submitted your thesis by the end of the 4th year, rather than having an option for a writing extension. Stipend funded PhDs will frequently, although not always, be linked to a specific research council funder, and may be linked with a research project grant awarded to one of the supervisors. Being aware of the funder can help you make decisions, as some funders provide enhanced networking and peer support to those that fall under their funding remit, as well as enhanced stipend levels, which can make these PhD programme both very attractive and competitive.

Unfunded PhDs, or self-funded PhDs, are generally where you approach a supervisor with an idea for a project you would like to undertake or develop. If you find a supervisor who is happy to support you and the development of your PhD topic, they will then help you put in an application for local university approval of your project and title. As the PhD is not associated with funding, you would need to cover not only your own living expenses, but also your annual academic fees and any other academic costs linked to the project. In a scientific PhD this would include things like bench fees and consumables, in other areas it may include covering conference expenses. If you are personally well resourced, this gives you the option of approaching a supervisor and co-development of your topic. A word of warning however, even if you can afford to follow this route it may be seen as less academically credible, as you won't have undertaken a competitive route in order to gain a place on a PhD programme initially.

PhDs undertaken as part of a training post may include a taught doctorate rather than a traditional research PhD. You may also find that your employer will pay your fees if the work you are already undertaking can be applicable to a PhD project. This means that the project costs are effectively covered, but that you will need to apply for additional funding to cover costs, such as conference presentations. These routes are not traditionally advertised but are developed in conjunction with your work place role. It may be worth discussing this route if you are applying for job roles where it may be applicable in order to see if it would be an option. There are also PhDs that are either fully or part funded by industry that may have an industrial placement requirement. These do tend be advertised via traditional routes and can be advantageous in terms of developing networks for future career opportunities. They may also provide access to specialist equipment or locations that would not be available via other routes, providing unique opportunities for specialist skill development.

Finally, the fellowship route is similar in some ways to a PhD undertaken as part of a training post, as it may be undertaken as part of a job role, although this is not always the case. A fellowship is where you apply to a research funder directly for funding to undertake a PhD, with the support of your workplace and/or university, and supervisors. It requires developing your own research question, gaining pilot data, calculating your own research costings, and frequently putting together your own training and development plan to enable your PhD to be a success. This route is probably the most competitive and requires substantial preparation, frequently over a year of working to pull everything together. On the other hand, it can offer a route by which you can undertake a PhD whilst still retaining your work place salary and have access to funding for training and consumables.

Each of these routes into a PhD have different pros and cons. If you don't have loads of money in the bank, then doing a self-funded PhD may not be an option for you. Other options, like a PhD with a stipend, may also be off the table if you are working and need your current salary to make ends meet. This in itself may determine which route you take. You may have resources in terms of finance but not in terms of time, you may therefore want to self-fund or do an unfunded PhD, in a way that enables you to stretch the process out over several years, so your annual time commitment is less. On the other hand, you may be time limited and need to get it done in the next 5 years, and therefore not have the time resource to put all your eggs into the same basket and apply for a fellowship that takes a year to prepare and has a 20% success rate. Being honest with yourself about your different drivers is essential so that you can make the right choices in terms of route.

There are other considerations which may impact your decision making in terms of fitting into your lifestyle requirements:

- Face to face or remote
- Full time or part time
- Overseas study requirement
- Industrial placement requirements
- Linkage to a doctoral school or other forms of strong peer support
- Support of additional learning requirements

Understanding how the routes you are interested in can best support your lifestyle is a crucial part of the decision-making process. It is important to undertake some in-depth research to understand which programmes can and cannot support your needs. You can find out more by looking at departmental literature, university handbooks, and details listed within adverts. You can also speak to individuals within departments, such as departmental post graduate tutors, who may be able to give more specialist guidance.

If you are looking at applying for routes that require more development, such as fellowships or self-funded routes, you should try to find others that have been through the process before. Different funders will have websites, and every grant application will contain guidance, but there are also often tips and tricks that are less well known or clearly articulated in easy to access information. You should also approach departments that are set up to support these kinds of applications, such as university research and development offices, or career departments, they should be able to offer you support in both choosing your approach and developing a proposal. Identifying supervisor support will also be an essential part of this process, so doing so early will reap rewards.

There is a PhD that is suitable for everyone, but not every PhD is suitable for all people. Don't just choose the route that you happen to know about, or the route that is most frequently available. Put in the time and effort to choose the route that will service you and your needs whilst maximising your future chances of success. Choose wisely now and you will thank yourself later.

CHAPTER THREE: CHOOSING THE RIGHT PHD FOR YOU

The truth of it is that all PhDs are challenging, and sometimes I think that achieving a PhD is more a measure of stubbornness and refusal to give up than of academic competence. There are however, some things that can be made much easier if you think about them and how they will work for you and your lifestyle before you embark on this particular journey. How much research have you done about what might be right for you? When I talk about research here, I'm not talking about the academic kind, I'm talking about fact finding and speaking to people type of research.

There are three main factors, in addition to PhD route, which you need to consider when selecting the right PhD for you:

- Project topic
- Supervision team
- Academic institution

The first thing people tend to jump to when thinking about choosing their PhD is the project topic. This is also the thing that will often come up with initial conversations with potential supervisors. You will often be asked what thinking you have done on your research question, and how far has it progressed? This thinking will tend to happen at different levels depending on the stage of application you are at and the PhD route that is applicable to you.

You may have:

- A broad subject idea, like Clinical Microbiology
- A more specific subject area, such as Gram-negative sepsis?
- Something really developed with a specific title, such as Comparison of Molecular Detection of Antimicrobial Resistance Mechanisms and the Impacts on Antimicrobial Prescribing Decisions?

If you are applying via a Fellowship route you will need to have a much more developed project, with aims and objectives thought through, alongside a title. If you are applying for a PhD advertised by a supervisor with pre-existing funding, they will already have a broad title that you need to understand and have thought about, but you won't be expected to have developed a project to the same level of thought. In which case you are probably using a broad subject area to identify initial options, and you will need to do further research when you decide to proceed further. Whatever happens however, by the time you decide to develop an application you will need to have formulated an understanding of the topic and a rationale for why this is an area you want to develop in, so fact finding and thought will be required.

Even if you are applying with a concept for a self-funded PhD, where you will have more self-determination, there are pros and cons about having reached different levels of thought development. It is good to leave enough conceptual room where your prospective supervisors can support you in ensuring that your research question is both achievable and of PhD level. Coming in with only the broadest level of thinking however, tends to imply you may not have thought about it enough and may limit how much support and sign posting someone can give you, as it will be harder to tell which funders might be interested or academically where it might sit.

Another consideration is who are you thinking of terms of supervision? Have you approached anyone? This step is often undertaken alongside your fact finding on possible projects, but many students see it as secondary to the actual topic itself. Making the right supervision decision is key however, not just in terms of topic but also in terms of your potential PhD experience. To put it bluntly, supervisors can either make or break your PhD experience, in many ways they are more important than your PhD topic, which will develop and change along the way. It is therefore always worth doing your due diligence in terms of understanding who is working in the subject area, but not just in terms of academic excellence but also in asking what is their working style? What is the experience of others in their department? Can they help you in the kind of career path you are envisioning for yourself? If you are undertaking a PhD linked to an existing career pathway, will they use their networks to not just assist you passing a PhD but to also support your career trajectory? How many of their students stay on with them after completion? For those that have moved on, where did they move to? Did they stay or leave academia? It can often feel strange trying to find out this kind of information, but when you are looking for a PhD you need to be looking to find the right fit for you and your future. There are many different ways and styles of supervision, and so you need to bear this in mind when you are reviewing your options.

Finally, you may also want to bear the institution in mind when selecting your PhD. How much weighting you place on this component will depend on your individual circumstances. It may be that your predominant influence is identifying your supervisors, with your institution being determined by those supervisors, and everything else becoming a secondary consideration. The reverse might also be true; with your supervision options determined by the institution you've selected.

Depending on your circumstances, and your geographic flexibility, it may be that institution, or location, is something you prioritise as a first line filter, over all other topics. Everyone's circumstances are different. Your options may be more restricted if you are looking at undertaking a PhD via a particular route, such as professional doctorate or combined clinical/academic placement. Sometimes, you may also have no choice in institution, especially if your studying is linked to a training scheme. In which case be aware of travel or other requirements when decided your route, as it may impact your experience. If you are limited to a single institution due to geography, or personal choice, there are still institutional considerations that you will wish to bear in mind. Most Universities, for instance, will have multiple departments that are offering PhD's within any given academic year, all of which may support your needs in different ways, and so there is still some thinking to be done.

If your institution options are less limited, there are many factors worth considering that may help you decide which institution works best for you. What kind of learning style do you prefer? Do you want close support and a lot of peers? These things need to be considered linked to the characteristics of institution you are considering. Would you be sitting within a small or large department? Are there multiple PhD students and post docs working in a similar area? What kind of requirements and support do they have across PhD programmes? If you have specific learning or other needs, can they support your specific requirements? I would advise, if possible, not just reading up about possible locations but also speaking to others about what it is like to study there. Talking to people will enable you to hear about the whole student experience, rather than just what's written in the academic brochure. Institutions, like supervisors, tend to have a specific style, and it may be one that works for you, but it also may be one that doesn't.

Depending on your end goal, your institution may also have more influence. If you want an academic career, you may wish to choose a university with higher perceived academic influence. Groups such as the Ivy League Universities in the USA or Russell Group Universities within the UK. Choosing an institution based on ranking or perceived academic excellence has pros and cons, and it really does depend on your why, which is why Chapter 1 of this book is so important. These universities often have access to higher levels of research funding and technology than their counter parts. If your aim is to stay on the academic path and attempt to get a post-doctoral position and attain your own research funding, their reputation and access to networks, are likely to help you maximise your chances of future options. The counter side to this, is that they are often more competitive and it can therefore be more difficult to secure an initial PhD place, not that being prepared to fight for success is a bad thing. They also tend to have more of a PhD factory approach, where you will be one of many students your supervisor has, and therefore their ability to individualise their support to you may not be so great. In reality, one institution isn't better than another, the best institution is the one that serves your learning needs and your future career aspirations. The one that will serve and align to your why, irrespective of name or ranking.

By approaching your PhD choice systematically, by considering: PhD topic, supervision team and academic institution, you can ensure that you have truly thought about the main aspects that may impact your PhD experience, and which factors mean the most to you. Not only putting in the thought, but also ranking these three different options will, I hope, help you navigate what can be a really intimidating process.

My suggestion is that you make a scoring matrix that has these three main areas and that then list five sub-categories populated by items, such as peer support, that may be important for you. Once you've got this, I would then weight the area and category that are most important and use this scoring matrix as an objective way of comparing your options. I am after all a scientist, and this is how my brain works. That said, be prepared to throw these scores out of the window and follow your heart and passion if you find something that really speaks to you, as it's this passion that will get you through your PhD no matter what gets thrown at you.

Head to the Girlymicrobiologist website for a template that can help you do this.

CHAPTER FOUR: DEVELOPING YOUR ELEVATOR PITCH

When I applied for my trainee Clinical Scientist post in 2004 there were 240 applications for 4 positions. The scheme has only got more competitive since then and PhD positions can be equally if not more competitive. It is therefore worth taking the time to think about what will enable you to stand out from the competition and make sure that you have a plan on how to clearly communicate this, both in writing and verbally to support your application.

For instance, are you applying for a PhD post and have already published papers, got a travel grant or partaken in research communication activity? Are you applying for a clinical PhD post and have already done work experience in a clinical lab, worked with patients or have a life experience that could help you? Ensuring you spend some time thinking and making a list of anything you have done or experienced that will enable you to stand out from the field will help you create your elevator pitch or a set of statements around your unique selling point, or USP.

Remember that PhDs are effectively graduate training schemes. These are first steps in a career that will last a lifetime and so having spent some time focussing on your why and by which route you want to go on that journey it is very important to know how to communicate effectively the results of your thinking to recruiters.

So how do you go about developing your elevator pitch?

There are several stages that can be helpful to go through in order to develop and then refine your elevator pitch. The first of which is to establish your USP, i.e. what is it that makes you, you?

There are several components to this, but one that I think can be a helpful place to start is think about what your personal core values are? What are the words that really sum up the core of who you are and what you believe in? Which three words really speak to you when looking through a list? These tend to be the words that if you can't enact or exemplify them make the world feel very unfair, or make you want to fight for the freedom to express them. For instance, my three core values are summarised by: collaboration, parity and independence. Yours are likely to be entirely different, but below are some example words that may help get you started on choosing yours:

Examples of words to describe personal core values:

Integrity	Authenticity	Accountability	Community
Respect	Citizenship	Creativity	Innovation
Equity	Honesty	Fun	Service
Boldness	Leadership	Influence	Kindness
Recognition	Curiosity	Competency	Growth
Autonomy	Stability	Independence	Optimism
Loyalty	Compassion	Security	Justice
Determination		Responsibility	

Once you have your three words, you'll want to move onto stage 2, which is making a list of the experiences or interests that sum up who you are and give a picture of the uniqueness that is you. This can feel a bit daunting at the start, so it's worth just getting two pieces of A4 paper and heading one, interests, and the other, experiences. Then just write down anything that springs to mind without adding any value judgements about whether what you are writing is good or bad. You will take plenty of time to review and refine this list later, for now it is all about just getting ideas down on paper.

Your experiences may be linked to a love of travelling, volunteering, undertaking the Duke of Edinburgh Award, a school trip or having attended a summer school. Examples of interests may include things such as playing music, playing video games, spending time with your friends, baking, or reading. Don't worry about whether these items seem grand or special, the most important thing is that they are genuinely things that you have really enjoyed.

Once you have your big lists, it's helpful to then go through and highlight things in a similar colour that group together by a theme. Do you have dancing, playing music and listening to music all down for instance, in which case highlight them under the theme of music. If you also have things like drawing, writing poetry, and performing, you could then cluster these and music together under creativity. Going through your lists in stages enables you to cluster items in larger and larger groups until you have a few key umbrella terms. You may, for instance, end up having one cluster under creativity, and another of self-development, linked to your listed interest in competitive sports, liking the gym, and enjoying taking evening classes.

At this point, it is always interesting to take a moment and see how much these align, or not, with the words you've chosen as describing your core values. They don't, and preferably won't be, the same words, but they hopefully combine to describe how your core values are enacted as part of your choices linked to how you live your life. For instance, my experiences and interests cluster around creativity, through writing and designing experiments. Exploration, through my love of travel, movies/TV, reading, cooking and museums. Gamification, as I love all things gaming, from computer games, board games and tabletop gaming, and finally connectedness, through my enjoyment of teamwork, spending time with close family and friends, and enjoyment of shared pursuits.

Once you have your three words that describe your core values and a list of terms that you can use to summarise your interests and experiences, as well as your 'why' from Chapter one, you then have the component parts to form the basis of your elevator pitch.

Your elevator pitch will be based on three USP linked bullet points:

- Who you are? – based on your core values
- Where you are now? – linked to your current interests and experiences
- Where are you interested in getting to? – this ties into your 'why' of doing a PhD

When you have your three bullet points, you should try and turn these into your pitch. Your pitch should aim for the 3 C's: clear, concise and compelling. It should tell the audience who you are as a person in simple, jargon free language, and when spoken aloud should take no more than 30 seconds to say. It should also, ideally, be an opening that is interesting enough to promote the listener to ask further questions to learn more and start a conversation. It can take quite a few iterations to get from your initial ideas down to a bullet pointed list, and it can take quite a lot more to get from a bullet pointed list to a three line paragraph that you are happy with. Once you've done it however, it should stand you in good stead for further developments on your curriculum vitae (CV), and for putting together your PhD applications. It is during your applications you will be able to expand more in detail, based on your original pitch, which you are likely to include at the start of your CV in order to help you stand out.

An example of an early draft:

"Hi, my name is Girlymicro. I'm applying for a PhD in clinical microbiology as I've always been passionate about working together with others to make breakthroughs that can help people, and clinical microbiology is a field that can really change people's lives. During my work experience I have seen that science is a creative space, where I was able to use my ability to see problems differently to add value to work that was already being undertaken. To build on this, I want to gain a PhD to prepare me to undertake better research, allow me to use my collaborative skills to build networks that will support impact, and gain enough experience to start developing a clinical academic career."

Once you have an initial draft then practice writing it. Each time you write it review each word and see whether that word is needed and think about whether it is the best choice of word to express your meaning. It is best to do this over time, with breaks in-between drafts. Then once you feel you have nailed it, I would walk away and leave it for a week or so, then come back and do another review. Sometimes, you need time and distance from your initial draft to identify if there is further work to be done to make it as impactful as possible. In the later stages it is also useful to gain external input from those that know you well, to help make sure you are not losing the essence of your USP through the drafting stage. It may sound counterintuitive, but things can be too perfect. Humans are not perfect and so neither will your USP be. You don't want to lose your individuality by making your pitch so polished it doesn't speak to who you are.

When you have your written pitch, you also want to ensure you practice speaking it. You may need to make some edits that differentiate what you will have in writing at the start of your CV, versus what you will verbalise when meeting people. You won't introduce yourself, for instance, at the start of your CV in the same way that you will when speaking face to face. When you practice speaking your pitch, make sure you pay attention to the delivery, not just the words. Think about making eye contact and ensuring your body language is open, no crossed arms etc. Also, practice avoiding common mistakes, such as tripping over your words because you are rushing, or being so eager that you speak so quickly no one truly hears what you have to say. Practice it so it feels natural, and you don't have to worry about remembering the details.

Don't hide who you are and have confidence that you have a lot to offer. Make sure your elevator pitch supports others in seeing you and all you can bring. Remember, you've done a lot of work to prepare your pitch so keep all of your notes, they will be useful when it comes to your full application. Approach applications using the same lessons as your pitch, grip your audience at the start, so that they will keep engaged and read on.

Head to the Girlymicrobiologist website for a template that can help you do this.

CHAPTER FIVE: PUTTING TOGETHER YOUR APPLICATION

Having spent some time thinking about your why, the type of PhD you want to do and how to talk about yourself (your USP), the time has come to put together your application. The first thing to really understand when you are writing an application for anything, but especially for a PhD, is what is being asked of you? A PhD application, although in many ways a job application, is also much more than that. It's less about where you are at right now and more about where you could be at the end of your studies. There's also a lot more in the assessment (application plus interview) about being able to demonstrate the way you think, your aspirations, and your passion. It's much more than the box ticking against a job specification that is often required for other types of posts.

PhD applications do vary in their requirements, but they commonly require two components, a cover letter linked to the reasons why you are applying for the job, and highlighting why you are a suitable applicant, and a CV, which lays out you educational, academic, and work experience, in order to back up your cover letter. Below are the kinds of things I want to see if I'm glancing over your application in order to put it in the consider pile:

- Why you want to do a PhD?
- Why this PhD?
- Why this subject or title?
- Why this supervision team?
- Why this university?
- What skills and experience do you bring
- How does this PhD align with your long-term goals

The first thing is to be specific when you are addressing any of the key points. Having looked at a lot of applications over the years for PhDs and other roles, my first big tip is that details matter. Making statements like 'I have good communication skills' won't tick the boxes of those reviewing your application. You need to have it followed up by a concrete example such as 'this was shown by me winning X poster prize at X conference' or 'me being asked to lead our group presentation on X, where we received a distinction'. Your examples don't have to be revolutionary, but you do need to back up your statement with something concrete. You are applying for a research post after all, so knowing how to evidence statements matters.

Before you start writing your application, take some time to sit down and make a list of possible examples to prepare. Let me be clear, no one expects you to have all the skills to do a PhD when you apply, otherwise you wouldn't be doing a PhD you'd be doing a post doc. That said, on the advert there will be some skill requirements that you will be expected to meet or be on the pathway to meeting. It's key that you cover these off in your application, either in the covering letter or CV. One of the key errors I find people make when putting together their applications is that they think all of the skills and experience listed must come from their scientific or academic backgrounds. This really isn't true, especially for an early career post. Leadership skills can be demonstrated from volunteer or other work experience, such as helping at Scouts or Guides. Conflict resolution skills can include things like bar work on a Saturday night. Time management could include how you helped your parents manage your 6 younger siblings when it came to after school activities. As part of you bringing your entire self to the post you should feel free to include all of the skills developed as part of the route that brought you to making the application.

It can be challenging to split out skills from experience, but if you have any, experiences can go a long way to demonstrating your commitment to the career you are hoping to embark upon. Have you attended seminars or other voluntary activities as part of your time at university? Have you arranged to shadow or undertake placements within a laboratory to gain extra experience? Did you engage in weekend or other field trips? These help to demonstrate interest, but they can also help to round out some of the short listers' understanding of what you may be bringing in terms of experience, and how that might benefit the initial phases of your PhD. I also always appreciate the way that applicants introduce items like these into the application, as it also helps me start to get a feel for how they think and approach challenges, which is one of the things I'm looking for to help an application stand out from the rest.

Have you had a volunteer role? Have you held a part time or other job role? Do you have a hobby or a life experience that really drives you? One application I recently reviewed, focussed on the applicant talking about how much they wanted to engage with dementia research as their grandmother had been in a care home linked to dementia, and they had personally witnessed the impact on their families. They then followed it up with information linked to dementia UK, showing they had both the drive and ability to find information. Applications are about bringing your whole self, so don't feel afraid to bring in examples from across your life experience.

Start by writing down a list of everything you can think of that might be useful for putting your cover letter and CV together. If you struggle to think of things, and I sometimes do, go through your calendar and see what you've got listed as part of your day-to-day activities. Think about the work you've submitted or academic work you've undertaken in the last 3 years, and how they could be used to evidence different aspects for your application. This is a necessary step for putting together your CV as well, so make this preparation serve double duty. Finally, just talking through the questions with friends and family may mean that they can help guide your thinking. Sometimes, just talking things through out loud can help.

After you have a long list, cluster it by putting it into the topics listed at the start of this chapter. Then turn your list into actual examples, by putting a sentence or two together that you can then modify based on the precise PhD you're applying for. It's easy to think you must be exceptional to succeed, but the truth is most of us aren't exceptional. We just have a passion, interest, or tenacity that gets us somewhere. Don't let yourself get talked out of backing your points up because your examples don't feel 'enough'. It is better to demonstrate that you know how to evidence, rather than choosing not to do so as you only want to use examples that are outside of the normal experience. Most supervisors will not expect you to have already published academic papers or been awarded academic prizes. If you have them great, if you don't use what you do have and focus on linking your examples in well with the requirements listed in the job description. When I'm looking at applications, I'm most interested in the person behind the grades and the details, rather than always caring who comes with the most outstanding CV.

Once you have your examples to help you structure your writing, it's time to start on your cover letter. PhDs are advertised all the time; your cover letter is therefore critical to help your application stand out from the rest of the pile. A generic letter that you've sent to 20+ options just won't cut it as most applications will receive tens to hundreds of applications to shortlist. A generic cover letter just won't pass the skim test. When I'm looking at applications, I want you to show me what makes you tick. How you think and approach challenges, and how you ended up sitting in front of a computer writing this application. This is why putting in your thinking about why you want to do a PhD and how to put that into an elevator pitch is important, before you ever sit down to write your application.

One of the top things you want to have jump out of your letter is why you think this particular PhD is the one you want to do. What is it about the topic that interests you? How does this fit in as a logical next step from what you've been doing so far? Where is your passion or interest in this topic? Your motivation, whatever it is, must be strong enough to get you through challenging PhD moments. Being able to describe it means your supervisor will be better able to understand how to support you in your future goals, and they can't do that if you don't know what those goals are. Anything generic is a real turn-off at this point. Make your statements demonstrate that you have chosen this PhD over any others, even if in reality you are applying for numerous options at the same time.

Another way you can show that you have researched and put thought into the process is by making sure you use the academic literature in developing your application. Ensure you reference a couple of key pieces of literature either linked to the PhD itself or published literature from the group or supervisors when you talk about why you are interested in working with them. If the PhD is funded by a particular funder, or through a particularly funded centre then I would also expect the application to reference what the funders remit is and what they aim to achieve. Demonstrating that you've taken the time to understand the context in which your research will be undertaken shows that you have the beginnings of the strategic awareness you will need to develop future funding applications during an academic career.

Most cover letters will focus on the topic of the PhD. The ones that really stand out however, will also include other relevant topics, such as why working with this supervisor is attractive to you. Supervisors make or break your PhD. It's the honest truth. Demonstrating you have awareness of how important this relationship is to your PhD goes a long way to show that you understand the challenge you are choosing to take on. I would always recommend reaching out to the primary supervisor ahead of applying therefore. You can then make an informed choice about whether this person will be the right support for you. Every supervisor has different styles and you as a learner have different needs. Understanding whether those two things will mesh is so important. You can then address why the supervisory team on offer is the right choice for you in your application.

The other thing that is worth including is why the university you're applying for is the right choice for you. Each university has a slightly different ethos or feel, so why does the one you are applying to match your requirements? Is it because it has an associated medical school or strong pre-existing links to local hospitals? Is it because you really like the structure of the PhD programme? Is that they have a doctoral school or other funding that links into a research council you are particularly interested in working with? It's always worth looking up what the PhD structure is like. Some will require you to submit regular essays, others will just have an ongoing log, still others will require you to start out by doing rotations or to take on additional academic modules to support your learning. Each university will have different upgrade windows, requirements and structures. State why this university works for you and your learning style. This not only makes it clear that you've done additional reading to understand the programme, but that you've also done the reflective thinking to see how you would fit into what is being offered.

Your CV is less likely to change as much as your cover letter between applications. It should, however, always be modified so that it reflects the skills list that is included in the advert and skill specification listed. Your CV can include non-academic aspects, such as volunteering, that will enable you to evidence how you meet the requirements. Your CV will have your academic experience as it's framework, but you then build out your CV from the same list that you utilised to develop your cover letter, based on the specific requirements of the role. Make the information in your CV related to the PhD proposal easy to find. Don't put down every technique or skill if only 25% of them are applicable to the topic you're applying for. Prioritise listing the relevant ones in detail and group the rest. You can then bring the others up at interview if appropriate.

Once you have your cover letter and CV written it is always worth asking someone else to read your application against the advertised requirements, preferably a non-expert, to get a neutral assessment of whether you have clearly covered off everything that is needed. Make sure you have delivered on what you have been asked for as more is not always better. If your combined letter and CV for a starting level post is more than 5 pages most reviewers will start to become less and less engaged. If you send more than 10 pages, many will not consider it for shortlisting. A key skill for a researcher is being able to engage with a question, shift information to identify what is relevant, and build an evidence-based response. If you send more than 10 pages, it signals that you are unable to manage at least one of these steps in an efficient manner and therefore cannot fully meet the person specification. So, ensure everything you include has purpose.

One final thing, use the opportunity of putting together your application and reaching out to your potential supervisors to really think through about whether this might be the right PhD for you. PhDs are the work of years and so making sure that you are choosing one that works for you is so much more than just getting selected for a programme. It is OK to use this process to develop your application skills, but before you say yes to an offer, be sure that you are signing onto the right PhD, not just any PhD.

CHAPTER SIX: PREPARING FOR YOUR INTERVIEW

You've been invited to interview for a PhD that really speaks to you, great news. You've done a lot of preparation to get you to this point, but you still need to do a little bit more in order to maximise your chances of success when you walk into the room. The good news is that you have already started by laying a foundation that you can build on. So, what other things can you do to prepare for your interview?

The first thing to do is look closely at the information you have been provided linked to the invite. Some PhD interviews are just that, interviews. Others will be more involved and may require a full day of different stages. This is often true for settings like a doctoral school, where they may be hiring 10s of PhD students for a programme at a single time. You may have been asked to prepare a presentation, or to select a paper to bring with you to discuss. It is important to go through the invite in detail to ensure you are not surprised.

There will also usually be contact details for the department and names of your interview panel, or others involved in the process. It is always a good idea to contact the department to see if you can visit ahead of time or speak to someone about the role, especially if you didn't do so in preparing your application. This will give you information you can utilise to make your answer preparation more specific, and to develop questions that are tailored to the post, for use when you are in the room. If you can visit, it also means that you have opportunities to speak to other people who may be future peers, such as other PhD students, who you might not meet otherwise. You can get a feel for the vibe of the department, and you can practice your journey, so that you have more information in planning your visit. You really don't want to run late because you discover it is really hard to actually find the department when you arrive at the university, so having a trial run, even if you can't do a full visit will help in your preparation.

Speaking of getting there on the day, have a plan and a backup plan. There is nothing worse than having to phone and say you will be late, and may not therefore be guaranteed a spot, or to arrive hot and panting, having lost your cool because of travel delays. Public transport can get cancelled, your car could break down, or if you're coming into London tube delays are a regular event. If you have pre-planned what you will do and looked into a variety of travel options you will be less stressed in the event of them actually happening. If you are going further afield, and can afford to, it is worth considering going the night before so you can have a chilled out interview day and not worry about travel impacts. If you are buying train tickets, and can afford to, it is probably better not to lock yourself into particular trains, as it can be stressful if the interview is taking longer than expected and you won't be able to make your return. I know it's a privilege, but if you can afford to build in flexibility it will be one thing off your plate. To help with this many universities will reimburse for travel, so make sure you ask as part of your preparations. Booking your travel early will also often help with the cost.

Another thing that is worth considering is your outfit. It can be really tempting to rush out and buy a new interview outfit that gets put into a cupboard and kept so that it remains perfect. Wearing something brand new can feel super nice. As someone who has turned up to a full day interview in what subsequently turned out to be the most uncomfortable outfit known to mankind, I wouldn't recommend this. It is worth wearing your outfit, and definitely the shoes, around the house for several hours before you have to wear it for the real event. You will then know if your top rides up, or your feet will be crippled within 30 minutes of putting on your shoes and make appropriate adjustments. You want to be focussed on the questions you are being asked, not worrying about the appearance of sweat patches during your interview. You will also want to consider the impression you want to make. It may be that you don't wish to turn up in a suit, but you may also want to reconsider turning up in trainers and your favourite jeans. Different settings will have different expectations, so dress to present the version of yourself you wish to put forward and align it with the setting you are trying to join.

When you receive an invite to interview for a post you will receive a whole bunch of information, some of which will be more apparent to you than others. There will be names listed, names of specialisms, names of the recruiting staff, all of which will give you a clue as to how to get information on the type of people who will be interviewing you. Use this information to re-visit the papers that you used during your application process and decide whether you want to include any others in your preparations. There may be a period of months between you applying and your interview, so also see if there are any new papers that would be especially topical in the area to ensure that you look like you have an up-to-date knowledge of the literature. This approach is especially important if you know you are going to be asked to bring a paper to discuss to the interview or that they are planning on giving all candidates the same paper to review. Think about what is good about the work, what are the limitations, and what you think about whether the paper has delivered on its aims and objectives. Practice summarising the key points in no more than 3 lines, so you can demonstrate your ability to prioritise information.

Whilst you are reviewing the papers you included in your application, you should also review you application more widely. As each of your applications will have been personalised make sure you know the one you submitted for this PhD in detail. You should also be prepared to expand upon your points. Concentrate on the desirables and make sure you have developed answers that will enable you to stand out in these areas, as everyone applying will meet the minimum specifications. When you are developing your answers try to also think about key themes that you want to communicate and embed throughout your interview. If you can, distil these themes down to three key words (e.g. experienced, enthusiastic, friendly) and use synonyms to utilise them in a variety of your answers when appropriate. This will help reinforce them to your panel.

You will want to also develop answers to some commonly asked questions. Always have an example of something you're not very good at/confident with, and a plan of how you're going to get better/feel more confident about it. Alongside all the things you're good at, of course. Think about how you will answer questions linked to how you will respond to challenge or failure, as well as how you deal with both individual and team working. Also, consider how you will answer questions linked to communication and learning styles, especially in how you might communicate to non-academics. Don't assume that all the questions asked will be technical or just linked to your PhD topic area. Make sure you take this opportunity to demonstrate your transferable skills and how your experiences up to this point will help prepare you for a PhD.

When you are preparing your responses to interview questions you might find it useful to use the STAR method of structuring them, Situation Task Action Result. This may help your answers to be specific, and to keep you focussed so you avoid drifting away from the question asked. For your answers explain what the situation was, so the panel understands the context. Discuss the task that you were trying to undertake, what were you trying to achieve? Give detail about the action, what did you do? Then finish with what the result of the action was. Depending on the question, you will want to cover what went well and what your learning from the scenario was. This structure will help with ensuring that you show, don't just tell.

Once you have your STAR responses it can help to practice giving them. This can enable you to build confidence, it can in turn also help you think about word selection. If you talk from a position of confidence rather than imposter syndrome, you will use words like 'will' and 'can', rather than using words like 'try' and 'attempt'. It seems a small change but there is a subconscious difference that is detected by the interviewer. When someone speaks in a definitive style it inspires confidence. It will not be the only thing that gets you across the finishing line, but it can definitely help. If you find this hard to do in isolation, then reach out to someone you trust. Get them to listen as you practice your elevator pitch & answers to support in both your delivery and help make your responses concise.

The final phase of preparation before the day is deciding on the questions you will ask of your interview panel. The one thing that many candidates don't come with, that could make them stand out, are questions linked to the research topic of the PhD they are applying for. When reading papers to prepare it is worth making note of questions that have sprung to mind, or anything that the PhD question itself has inspired. You can then ask some of these, if the opportunity arises during an interview. Demonstrating this kind of research curiosity can often make the difference by enabling you stand out from the other candidates. You should also prepare a few questions on the setting and opportunities for the end of the interview, when you will be asked if you have any questions. This is the moment when you can also ask the questions that will enable you to judge whether this is the right PhD for you but be careful to ask open questions that demonstrate curiosity, rather than ones that will only elicit yes/no answers only.

Once you're at the day itself, you have done all the preparation, you have sorted your travel, you know what you are going to wear, the only thing left to focus on is being present in the room during the interview itself. Your aim is to make the interview feel more like a conversation than an interrogation, and it's OK to be nervous, everyone is expecting you to be. What you might not realise is that it is also normal for your interviewers to be a little bit nervous also. I once famously over gesticulated when I was interviewing for a PhD student and gesticulated so wildly that I threw tea everywhere as I caught my cup. Luckily, we all laughed, and the interviewee was not put off accepting a PhD with me.

When you walk into the room, it's worth always making sure that there is a drink of water available. If you are doing a remote interview, make sure you have one prepared, even if you think you won't need it. There is nothing worse than being very distracted by a sudden thirst and not having a way to address it. Water can serve a wider purpose though. It can buy you time if you need a moment to think through a tricky question being asked. It can provide you with a nice way to pause before answering, so that you can formulate a more structured STAR response. In general, even if you have an immediate answer, it is good to take a second before responding to any question. It can help you ensure you are about to answer the question they have asked, not the question you think they've asked. It also helps ensure you don't let the headlong rush of words trip you up when you are trying to answer. Taking a sip of water or starting a phrase with ""That's a good question" will show you are thinking and taking the interviewers questions seriously.

If you've been asked to prepare a presentation, make sure that you have sent it on ahead of time, to the deadline they have set. Make sure that you also have it with you on a USB stick, and it may even be worth printing copies and putting them in files for each of your interviewers to demonstrate your level of preparation. If you have been given a time limit for the talk, make sure you have practiced ensuring that you will not exceed the time limit. I would try to exclude animations, videos or anything that may be a source of difficulty on the day if it doesn't play correctly. You don't want to add to your stress in the moment. If you've been asked to bring a paper, try to print it out and offer it to your interviewers in the same way. It's a personal touch that can help develop rapport. It is OK to bring notes with you into the room, but if you can it is better to try and not utilise them, this is true for the questions, as well as any presentations or papers.

You will often be offered a tour on the day, either before or after your interview. If you haven't managed to visit ahead of time, and if the tour is before the interview, this can also provide you with additional information that may help enhance your interview responses or questions you plan to ask. It is worth knowing that this may not just be a tour, however. These interactions with future peers or colleagues can often be reviewed by the panel as part of the overall assessment process. Panel members may ask those leading the tour to provide their assessment of how you acted and how you would fit into the department. Sometimes these informal assessments are the things that make the difference in choosing between candidates that have performed equally well in the formal interview process.

My final tip is this, have some faith in who you are and your ability to succeed. You have achieved so much to get you to the point where you are qualified to apply for a PhD. You deserve to give yourself the same self-belief and encouragement that you would offer friends and family if they were in same situation. Remember that, in any job interview, you are interviewing them as much as they are interviewing you. They want you to be a good fit. To solve the problem they have of needing someone, but equally, you can decide if they are a good fit for you. Don't just accept any PhD. Don't just accept the first offer you receive. Make sure you accept the right one for you. You are after all, worth waiting for.

TOP TIPS FOR GETTING STARTED ON YOUR PHD JOURNEY

Hi, I'm Sam, and I was one of Elaine's PhD students until I graduated in 2025. As part of her prep for this book she asked me to write a piece to share some of the things I learnt along the way that might help someone starting out on their PhD journey. I hope that you find this helpful, and that you enjoy your PhD as much as I enjoyed mine.

What I wish I knew before starting a PhD

Having an understanding of what the process of doing a PhD is actually like can be invaluable when starting off on the PhD journey. I was in a strange position where I always knew I wanted to do a PhD. I loved the idea of being able to do research in an area that I found fascinating, that being microbiology. Despite this, when I was starting off on my university journey back in 2015, didn't really have any idea what the PhD process would actually be like. I knew that they were an opportunity to explore a research topic and would involve writing a thesis and passing something called a 'viva'. In first year of my undergraduate program however, the PhD journey felt suitably far away to not worry about. Now I am on the other side of the process, there are some aspects of the PhD process that I think would have been incredibly useful to know about before I applied – or aspects to have been aware of going in.

The supervisor-student relationship

I always thought that the most important aspect of embarking on a PhD was he topic of research. Naturally, you won't be motivated to complete the journey if you are researching a topic that you don't have that innate passion for. What I didn't pay much attention to beforehand however, was the importance of having a good working relationship with your supervisors. Admittedly, this can be quite hard to gauge before you actually start on a PhD, as your contact with the supervisors will likely be limited to an interview for the position. But, where possible, it is absolutely worth researching your supervisors when applying. Have a look at their research outputs. What topics do they research in and outside of the specific area that the PhD project you are interested in? Do they work across disciplines? How large is their research group? Do they do any public engagement or outreach activities? There is no set of 'right' answers to these – it all depends on your own working style and where you see yourself fitting in. If you value having regular contact with your supervisory team, then a large research group may not be best for you. Equally, smaller groups may not give you the same breadth of exposure to other areas of research. And again, these are not hard-and-fast rules, but understanding the way your supervisors work and the dynamics of their team is essential to ensuring you get the most out of your PhD. You are signing up for three-four years of work with them after all.

There are more options than you think

As I mentioned, I always knew I wanted to do a PhD. This is because the idea of research greatly appeals to me, but also because I thought that a PhD was the only way to do this. Now, this isn't to say that a PhD wasn't right for me – it absolutely was – but I didn't even know what the other equivalent qualifications were. I only found out what a doctoral fellowship was late in my first year of my PhD. Having a broader understanding of the options available is incredibly important, both in identifying all the opportunities out there, but also in helping you refine what you want to get out of the process. It may well be the case that you research all the available avenues and you decide that a 'traditional' PhD is the right option for you. But by looking at the other avenues available may well help you identify a better route for you to pursue your doctoral-level education through. Ultimately, the PhD journey is an incredibly personal one, and you should choose the pathway that is right for you in terms of how you learn, where your passion lies and what you want to do after your PhD is completed.

The financial aspect

This can often be the elephant in the room when it comes to PhD programmes. There is no denying that at times the finances around PhDs can be a challenge. The available funds for your project and pay will vary based on the type of doctoral programme you are on and on the nature of the research. Having a better understanding of the financial aspects behind the PhD process would have been very helpful for me before I started my PhD journey. If applying for a funded PhD, you may be able to find out what the expected pay is. There is also aggregated information online on average PhD stipends, which can help you with any financial planning you need to do prior to the PhD starting. Bear in mind that stipends may vary based on location – London universities will pay a higher stipend due to London adjusted wages. Understanding this ahead of time will help plan how you will support yourself through the process. Will the stipend be sufficient to support you? Do you think you will need to take on a part-time role to help (this is what I did for two years during my PhD)?

On an aside, if you decide that you will do additional part-time work, just be wary of the toll this may take on you. PhDs are hard work and can be very tiring – make sure you leave enough time to rest and relax. Another aspect to consider here is everyone's favourite topic – tax. Stipends are tax-exempt, which means they do not count towards your taxable income. This is something to be aware of if undertaking part time work – it is worth calculating how much you will be earning from any additional work and establishing if you will be over the tax threshold. Also, if you undertake any self-employed work, such as tutoring, then be aware of any requirements to declare these earnings. HMRC has several useful resources to help you unpick this, and if you are unsure then giving them a phone call can be useful in establishing what your obligations may/may not be.

It's okay to step away

There are points where doing a PhD can feel like too much. This probably happens to everyone, but I found it quite difficult to deal with when it happened to me. When the pressure is really on, I tend to hyper-focus in on the task, which is not always beneficial. It can feel like the only option, but doesn't always lead to the best work. What my supervisors told me to do is, once in a while, just step away. For me this felt like the complete opposite thing to be doing. When deadlines are looming, stepping away can feel like the absolute last thing to do. But in the world of PhDs, which ultimately are a very creative process, taking time to step back is essential. I found that not only would it help calm me down, it would also actually improve my productivity when I would start up work again. Whether I went for a walk in the local park, or went to the café, or decided that I was actually going to take some holiday, having those breaks would help me feel refreshed, de-stressed and ready to make constructive progress. I think this may be more of a 'I wish I knew before embarking on a large project' rather than a PhD-specific piece of knowledge, but I think it is still valuable. Having the time to reflect and process, even if it is subconscious, can help clarify situations, generate and build on new ideas and allow you to tackle problems from new angles. This is especially useful when writing your transfer thesis and final thesis. Spending days on end writing can be exhausting, so having breaks is key to keep momentum going.

Dr Sam Watkins - 2025

SECTION TWO – HOW TO SURVIVE AND THRIVE DURING YOUR PHD PROGRAMME

YEAR ONE

CHAPTER SEVEN: GETTING OFF TO THE BEST START

The start of a big project, like a PhD, is incredibly exciting, but it can also be stressful, intimidating, and result in anxiety. If you don't start in the right way, it can feel like that the whole thing will be lost before it even starts. This, of course, isn't true, but starting in the best way possible can make these initial stages easier. You've done a lot of planning and preparation to get to this moment, and so moving forward in the same way will stand you in equally good stead.

Let's start with that impostor syndrome. Let me tell you, it's never about being the smartest person in the room. When I first started in my role as a trainee Clinical Scientist, and then as a PhD student, I just remember being overawed by everyone in the room. Everyone had amazing titles, years of experience and just an aura that suggested competence and knowledge. I would look at my fellow PhD students and compare myself. This is one of the things that most commonly happens with my students even now. They benchmark themselves against other people, other projects, other networks. Now, benchmarking is fine, and we'll talk more about that in other chapters, but only if it helps you plan and move forward, not if it causes you self-doubt. Everyone starts a PhD at a different point and for different reasons, this is reflected in the number of routes into PhDs that are available. It is almost impossible to truly compare yourself to anyone else because of this. Your journey is your own.

It took me a long time to understand that my contribution wasn't about being smarter than anyone else, I've never felt like the smartest person in any room. Your contribution will be about offering a new perspective that is unique to you. Sometimes that's from a technical or academic point of view. Sometimes that will be by who you can connect the people in the room with. Sometimes that will be by offering a different lens through which the situation can be seen, being new to an environment means you will be able to review things without historical bias. You have been chosen to be in the room however, so don't let that self-doubt impact how you take your first steps.

One of the reasons it's worth taking the time to start your PhD with confidence is because, to make the most of the opportunity, you will need to put yourself out there and do things that may make you feel uncomfortable, like asking questions. Asking questions frequently and of all of the different people you will encounter is a crucial part of demonstrating curiosity and learning. Trust me there are no stupid questions, no matter how it may feel to you in the moment.

I love people that ask questions, it makes me think, it makes me remember why I've made decisions and assess if they are still relevant. When I started out, I was worried that asking questions would just demonstrate my ignorance. It takes courage to ask questions and to be part of the discussion. As a supervisor it is very difficult to evaluate whether you are covering knowledge gaps or pitching what you are doing correctly if the dialogue is one way, so students that engage and query are a blessing. As a PhD student you are there to learn and to break new ground, so as your confidence grows it is also good to question and challenge. There are many different ways of doing things and only by having dialogue can you really understand why certain decisions get made under some circumstances and not in others. If you are an introvert and not comfortable asking questions openly, make notes, email and discuss your findings, find a way that works for you and for your mentor. Constructive questioning is a skill that you will need throughout your career, so starting to develop this skill set early will reap earlier rewards.

All those questions will come with a lot of information; you will also be given a lot of details in general when you start and are trying to find your feet. The start can feel like information overload. One of my biggest tips is to make copious notes, whether you think you will remember the information or not. I would make notes of not just the information itself, but of the things you don't understand, or the further questions that the details prompt. Some of the information may not feel relevant but may be invaluable later. Some of it you may feel like you have a good grasp of in the moment, but will probably lose some understanding of later, as time goes on you are receiving so much data in a short period of time. Some of the things you don't understand will form the basis of your first foray into the literature and give you a sense of direction rather than just randomly reading.

The other advantage of taking notes, over helping you sort through your feeling in the moment, is that by reviewing notes when you come back to something, after a break or temporary focus elsewhere, you will be able to make connections which may not have been obvious to you the first time around. It will also enable you to ask questions better and have more enriched meetings with your mentor/trainer/supervisor as you will have access to specifics that you've come back to. Plus, when you look back at your notes from 10 years ago it will make you realise how far you've come and how much you have achieved.

It may feel early to say this, but the purpose of a PhD is to become an independent researcher, and this is something to bear in mind right from the beginning and develop a focus on being the master of your own destiny. Every trainee/student is different. Hopefully you will get a supervisor who will have the time to help you reflect on your learning needs, but you need to also be able to develop the skills to do this yourself as you won't always have access to someone to do it with you. Most training programmes are quite structured but there are always many ways to deliver on the same learning outcomes. This is a career, and every career journey is personal, so the sooner you can get into the habit of thinking about what your strengths and weaknesses are, and what your specialist areas of interest could be, the more you will get out of any opportunities you are offered. Within academia you will often not be offered opportunities on a plate, but if you know what you want and find the opportunity, you will very rarely get blocked from accessing them. Start thinking early about what could enrich your training and find ways to access those experiences. Get into the habit of developing your self-reflection skills and acting on the results. You can't do everything all at once but embed addressing your gaps in your project plans from an early point.

Sadly, anyone who tells you that a PhD is 9 – 5 Monday to Friday is lying, but you can do one and still have a life. I've sat in a lot of lectures from very senior people who talk to trainees about academic work not being 9 – 5, it's true but in many ways, this saddens me. It gets spoken about as if you can't have a life, you either choose devotion to this vocation, or it isn't for you. There will definitely be times where you need to commit more than the standard hours, when you have a data collection deadline, or are writing your thesis etc, but this shouldn't be the norm. I encourage my students to take on extra curricula activities, such as public engagement, which often happen on the weekend, but this is a few times a year. Training shouldn't be about burn out. To fully learn and develop it is crucial to have the mental space to reflect and plenty of recovery time. You need to find strategies early on that work for you in order to manage your time. Do you want to block out every Friday afternoon for paper reading? If you do need to put in some extra hours, would you rather do it at your desk to maintain work home separation, or work on the sofa. Be aware early on of working to manage stress rather than to manage task and develop strategies to enable yourself to walk away and unwind. You should be able to foresee and schedule in your work heavy periods and therefore be able to manage the peaks and troughs whilst ensuring you also have time for yourself when the workload or deadlines are not so immediate.

Three years, or a bit longer depending on your programme, feels like a long time when you start but it's not really. Before you know it, you will be 18 months in and needing to start thinking about what the next stage of your career may look like. As part of your progress, it is therefore important to make sure you regularly check in with yourself about what you've enjoyed and your aspirations to make sure you're on track for the career you want. The more you do this, the more you will be able to mould your training around the experiences and networks you will need to help you succeed. A lot of us fall into career choices, but if you can be deliberate, it will help you find happiness as well as success.

One thing that can help with ensuring strategies for future success is making sure you take the opportunity to make connections and put yourself out there right from the start. Finding opportunities often depends on knowing the people who are making them or have access to them. This is often difficult when you are starting out in a new field or career as you don't know who the right people are to signpost you to your available options. This goes for job posts, as well as learning and accessing skills. There are now some ways where you can do this on your own, such as social media, which are less reliant on introductions. It is worth considering how you can use your USP and the elevator you spent time creating as part of developing an internet presence, both to help yourself, but also to help other aspiring PhD students. There are other routes that can also help early on, join your professional body, find a trainee network, engage in public engagement, go for coffee with your fellow PhD students. Relationships and connections forged now will pay dividends later and are worth the investment, even if you are busy with other things.

Finally, despite the overwhelm, and hopefully exciting chaos of the start, make sure you take time to enjoy the ride. I was so focused on the end goal that I didn't enjoy the journey as much as I should have. I know I've said that you need to keep one eye on the future, and that's true, but being early in your career gives you a freedom to make decisions and enjoy experiences you just won't get later. Learning is your focus right now, free of the demands of the inbox, meetings and other peoples' agendas. Make sure you relish every moment as you will have less and less time to just enjoy learning as your career progresses.

CHAPTER EIGHT: DEVELOPING YOUR LEARNING AGREEMENT

PhDs can often be idealised as experiential learning, the reality of them can be very different however, your experience can depend very much on the environment you are in and the supervisor who is your predominant point of contact. It is easy to end up being a passenger, and passive in the process. I've talked previously about the importance of being the master of your own destiny, this is a key example of something that you can proactively undertake early on that can substantially change your PhD experience. I hadn't even heard of a learning agreement when I was a PhD student, in fact they are something that I discovered relatively recently, but they have really changed the way I handle the initial 'getting to know you phase' that I go through with a new PhD student. As I've seen the benefits, both for my students, and for me as a supervisor, I thought it was worth dedicating a chapter to talking about what they are, how they can help, and the process for putting one together.

So, what is a learning agreement and why is taking this time worthwhile? Surely everyone knows what they've signed up for when they take a training place. In general, I think most of us are good about talking about the nuts and bolts of what a course/placement entails when someone starts. We are good at giving the 'this is the bathroom' tour and 'this is where your desk is' plus 'our supervisor meetings are on Tuesday' type of information. The truth of the matter is that PhD students often know the logistics of what they've signed up for, but any learning placement is a whole lot more than just the nuts and bolts of what happens to deliver the thesis.

What I have discovered over the last few years is that imparting curriculum or logistic based information just isn't enough to support a good supervisor-learner relationship, where both get what they want out of it. As a PhD student coming into an environment that may be pretty alien, it can initially feel like you are floundering. It can feel like, right from the start, you don't fit. This is often combined and amplified by the fact that you may have moved or lost your support networks in the transition to starting a PhD programme. A small percentage of students walk away from their PhD programmes because of this, not really understanding the cause. This is such a travesty and something that can be addressed early on by having good conversations between supervisor and student.

From a supervisor/learner perspective, most problems occur when a disconnect between expectations and reality occurs on either side. Problems which could have been easily addressed early on develop into what can feel like insurmountable obstacles. These can have significant impacts on learner experience and supervisor stress levels if only discovered later, when the challenges can be much more difficult to address. There is a lot of expectation setting/management required at the start of any big project, let alone a PhD, but sometimes, by focussing on the logistics rather than the wider context, some of this expectation setting and sharing get missed.

In light of these complexities how can a learning agreement help? Well, they take quite a few different forms depending on what it is that you want them to fulfil. The common theme amongst them all is that a learning agreement is based on conversations between the learner and their supervisor where they both actively set out the expectations and boundaries of their relationship.

They can include all kinds of things:

- What topics are in or out of the learning objectives
- How deadlines will be set and a broad plan of work
- Expectation setting around students identifying additional learning objectives
- Ideas for how the learner will benchmark their progress and/or learning
- How the educator will assess progress/learning

In short, they are about making the implicit, explicit. Although the above questions are often part of most frameworks, the most valuable parts of a learning agreement, for me, are less structural and I always work to include these. It's your time to reflect and discuss:

- What kind of learner are you?
- What kind of support do you prefer
- What are your main objectives that may or may not be topic based?
- What are you hoping this will lead to?
- How do you prefer to communicate, face to face, email etc?
- Why this course? Why this training? What attracted you? What

would you like to get out of this opportunity, outside of a PhD?

As supervisors we often expect learners to be able to undertake independent study at the point of entering a PhD programme, identifying their own learning objectives and being responsible for any escalations. If this is your first post graduate experience, however, you may assume it will follow the pattern of the prior learning you have experienced, which may have placed a lot more focus on structure and consistency. Undergraduate, or even some post graduate master's level study, are very different in terms of both structure and expectations compared to a PhD programme. For instance, at first, many PhD students won't be used to maintaining their own goal setting and motivation outside of a structure that is delivered to them.

To begin this process of adjustment reflection is key, both based on your previous experience as a learner and linked to your goals that you wish to achieve during your programme. It starts by thinking about what kind of learner you are. You also need to think about what your needs are. Do you need a supervisor who is going to have a lot of pastoral time? Do you want to be in a group with plenty of other PhD students, so you have access to peer support? Do you hate micromanagement and pretty much want high level accessible support when you need it, but a light touch the rest of the time? These things will determine what kind of conversation you need to have with your supervisor in order to ensure that you have discussed the kind of support that may be most appropriate to you and will aid you in making the best start that you can.

As a PhD student just starting out you often won't have the same implicit and organisational knowledge as your supervisor, who will have often been working for a long time. It can be even worse if your supervisor is new, and you are the first PhD student they have had, as they will be learning how to be a PhD supervisor on the job with you. In general, supervisors have quite a lot of expectations that they don't necessarily voice. It can therefore be easy to for them to make assumptions about the level of awareness of these expectations from someone coming into a supervisor-learner relationship. As I've said before, PhD students will all start at different places due to prior experience and personal interests, and so using learning agreements can enable structured discussions to establish where each individual is starting from, and what kind of personalised support may be needed. Unless we all work together as a supervisor/learner pair to make things that we implicitly understand explicit, we won't know where the differences between practice and expectations lie.

Having these conversations can feel uncomfortable and challenging, mostly because of the fear of the unknown. They may also take time that is difficult to secure with your supervisor. All of these are reasons to make sure it is done correctly and given the time required. So how do we hold these conversations and support them getting the best outcomes? Before you meet you should decide with your supervisor:

- Clear objectives, what are you both trying to achieve
- What's included or not i.e. inclusion of pastoral support
- Timeframe for prior access to the learning framework
- Dedicated time in an uninterrupted space
- Clear timelines, as more than one meeting may be required
- Ground rules, such as approaching all points with openness and curiosity, to support open sharing

Crucially, know that it's OK if the outcome of these conversations is that your learner/supervisor styles don't match. This isn't about any one style or process being better than any others. By knowing early where any disconnect occurs you work together to find the best route forward, signpost to things that might help, and find additional support to ensure that the learning process itself still works.

What other things should you consider?

- Where should you have the meeting?
- What framework will you use? Does your university have one that you can utilise?
- Is this something your supervisor has done before?
- Talking through the questions with people who know you well before hand to aid reflection

Once you've had the initial conversation, you will want to ensure that you have set a date for when you will review what you've discussed. Your learning needs in year one will be very different to your needs and support requirements in year two, and they will change again during writing up and prior to submission. Your PhD is there to support your growth and so should change and flex to continue to stretch, but also support you, as you grow into being an independent researcher. It is also worth thinking about the timing for your initial meetings. You will probably want to undertake the discussion over several sessions, not just because they can take some time, but because there are probably a lot of things you don't really know during your first week in post. It is only by trying out some experiences and being within the setting to realise you have questions that this process can become the most useful.

Head to the Girlymicrobiologist website for a template that can help you do this.

CHAPTER NINE: MANAGING YOUR SUPERVISOR

All relationships require work. All relationships, especially ones that last years, will go through peaks and troughs. Your relationship with your supervisor is no different, and because of this, communication is key. This sounds easy enough, but sadly, it is often not. Finding the balance between being that student who needs supervisor input into every thought/decision, meaning you don't find independence, and being that student who never speaks up and therefore ostriches on issues, meaning that issues don't get addressed, is not an easy one. It requires the pair of you to build trust, and that is a gradual process.

I talked in section one about researching your supervisors in order to be able to talk about their work and department. In all honesty, though, there is a much stronger reason to start early on understanding your supervisor. They can make or break your experience during your PhD. I've been on both sides of the fence. I've been the PhD student who couldn't get time with their supervisor and the Clinical Scientist trainee who just wanted to be included. I am now the PhD supervisor whose diary looks like a train wreck and who feels constantly guilty about not having enough time to devote to those whom she's training. Undertaking a learning agreement can be a great way to start understanding your supervisor better in order to maximise your relationship, but supervisor management is something that you won't just need to try at the start of your relationship, but throughout your PhD.

One of the biggest changes when you start a PhD is that it is your PhD. You are in the driving seat. I struggled at various points during my own PhD because I didn't start off understanding that there was a requirement to curate and nurture the supervisor/student relationship, to actively manage my supervisor. A PhD is effectively a job, and the switch up to the responsibility sitting with you can be a challenging shift. No one is policing deadlines, and in fact, you are the one that should be setting them, even if your supervisor is there to help. No one is prioritising your workload. You need to work out, with support, what needs to come first at any given time. The lesson about not being passive is important across all aspects of your PhD. You are no longer in a taught process.

A PhD is effectively an apprenticeship in research, and like in any job, there are expectations placed on the employee in terms of delivery and performance. The earlier you can come to terms with this and start practicing goal setting, the easier your pathway will be. Supervisor management includes paying attention to how your supervisor works, in order to maximise the outputs of your relationship. Every supervisor is different, just like every person is different. The more you know, the better placed you are to understand what the dynamics of your relationship might look like, and importantly whether there are any possible pitfalls which you could then address early, preventing then becoming something more. In this one, knowledge really is power. So, get as much knowledge as you can as early as you can.

The first thing to tackle is finding out their working patterns and working preferences so you can ensure that you establish your communication patterns early. Are they someone who likes drop-in visits, or has standard office drop-in hours, or are they like me i.e. if it isn't in the diary it won't happen. Learn how to support the supervision process by keeping notes from your meetings and emailing them after your session to your supervisor, both for record keeping/prompts and to aid reflection. Finally, take the time to think about what you want from each face to face to make sure you maximise your time.

So much communication these days won't be face to face however, a lot of it will be digital. My inbox is the place where emails go to die, and my diary is a horror show. These are facts. No matter how much I try to keep on top of it, I get hundreds of emails every day, and to be honest I can't keep up. If you only send me a single email, it will get lost. I therefore ask my students, if it is important, to email me three reminders and make it high priority. This vastly increases the chance that I will see it and therefore will do the thing that I'm needed to do. If my students want to see me every two weeks, then let's get a regular slot in, which will move, but at least it's there. All of this is not because I don't care, it's just the only way I can manage multiple competing priorities. Everyone is different. You will have your own way of working, as will your supervisor. There is no point in being passive in the process and miserable about the outcome. You will have needs, and you have to actively work to find the best way that they can be met.

A lot of this is helped by laying the groundwork and having open discussions about expectations. Being open to supportive feedback, asking questions, and owning your work by doing things like reading and coming prepared to meetings goes a long way towards making these relationships flourish. Also, being transparent about challenges and identifying issues early can mean that both sides are facilitated in addressing issues. Your supervisor can't help if they don't know.

One of the things that can help with adjusting to this very different kind of environment is to understand the rules. That's both the formal written rules and the informal social academic rules. It's only by knowing these that you can judge whether any challenge or breakdown with your supervisor is precipitated by a valid breach. If you don't know the rules, how can you tell if you've broken them? A supervisor/learner relationship is always going to be based on an agreement to deliver, and if you have broken the rules by not delivering, for instance by repeatedly missing meetings or deadlines, then we all need to act like adults, hold up our hands, and seek forgiveness whilst taking corrective action. The other reason to know the rules is that you may need the information they provide to support your planning and to help in this delivery. Having access to details about university processes can be really useful in finding support when you need it, but also in undertaking goal setting and helping you meet your supervisors' expectations.

I'm going to also briefly cover here the opposite issue to having a supervisor that you don't feel you can connect with, the supervisor who you really click with. There are still rules here too, the main one being that being friendly is not the same as being friends. We all hear great tales of supervisors and students being best friends. I'm sure that happens after the PhD is over, but I've never known it happen during. I'd like to say I get on really well with my students. I'm invested in them. I care about them. I will happily buy them a beer in the pub. We are however not friends. My wellbeing is not on them. It is not an evenly balanced relationship. I am there to support them, but I am also their boss. In a friendship, if we went to the pub, my friends and I would take turns buying in rounds and discussing our problems. I'm pretty open about my work-based challenges, but I don't expect my students to take them onboard. I don't ever expect them to buy me a drink. I personally don't think that's how these things should work. When they are done being my students, when I no longer have responsibility for them, then the relationship can become more bi-directional. Until then I have a duty of care which means I should put them first. This is important to keep in mind as maintaining a professional relationship will make it easier for you to raise any concerns you have, or that your supervisor has with you.

Because of the significance of the supervisor/student relationship on your chances of PhD success, you should always be prepared and have a plan B. No matter how happy you are, no matter what stage you're at, I think it's a sensible approach. Hopefully, you will never need it, but strategic thinking is a good skill to develop regardless. You should always have more than one supervisor, even if the others have variable involvement. This is for practical reasons, as supervisors can get sick, or other life events can happen that makes them less available. If you can, it's always worth trying to include your additional supervisors in some of your meetings and investing in developing relationships with them as well. They can provide a counterpoint view on your work, and they can help with benchmarking your relationship and expectations with your primary supervisor. Your secondary supervisor is also likely to be involved at times, such as your upgrade viva, and so understanding their expectations can be really helpful. In the unlikely event that your relationship with your primary is not great, they can also take on a mediation role to help both sides gain clarity and hopefully move forward. If you hope for the best and plan for the worst, you should have all sides covered and hopefully have the most fulfilling experience possible during you PhD.

Finally, it's worth remembering that supervisors are people too. They have good days and bad days. They have personal stuff going on that can impact their mood, availability and decision-making. They will make mistakes and hopefully apologise for them. They will aim for perfection and always fall short. What I hope more than anything is that you will find a supervisor who wants and drives for you to reach your potential and who always has your best interests at heart. Sometimes, that means that there will be hard conversations, and sometimes that means they will push you, as they have faith in your ability to improve. I want all of my students to grow to be better than I am. I want them to know that I have faith in them even when they feel lost and can't find faith in themselves. Investing in your relationship will pay dividends and result in the best outcomes for both of you. So, despite the start of your PhD being a whirlwind, with so many things to do, make time to invest in a relationship that has the potential to really impact on your overall success.

CHAPTER TEN: DEVELOPING YOUR GOAL SETTING SKILLS

A PhD is the biggest single project that most people will ever manage on their own as a continuous piece of work. It feels like a huge undertaking, and it can often feel overwhelming. Like any project, therefore, it benefits from being split into more manageable chunks. As so much of your success and wellbeing during a PhD is based upon you setting regular goals, it's worth spending some time thinking about what a good goal might look like.

As you'd probably expect, I spend a lot of my working life talking to people about goals, be they personal or organisational. I've also spent the last 20 or so years setting good goals and also setting some truly dreadful ones, either because they were unachievable or developed in a way that just wasn't helpful. To counter this, you will hear an awful lot about how goals should be S.M.A.R.T.:

- Specific: Targeting a particular area for development or task
- Measurable: They should include a predefined indicator of progress
- Assignable: If your goal requires support, who from and what do you need
- Realistic: Defined with attainable results within available resources
- Time-related: Include a timeline for expected results

These principles can make goal setting sound really complex, and like their development will take a whole bunch of time. That can definitely be true if you are setting things up for a big piece of work or a project. The principles can however also be applied to more modest goals that aren't about big things. For instance, if I manage to do a 20 minute block of writing right now, I will reward myself with a pot of the pink earl grey tea I currently love so much. Therefore, getting into a habit of thinking what is achievable and embedding specificity, even into the little things, is a good routine to get into.

Let's start with the specific component of goal setting. Your goals must never be things like: 'write a chapter', 'write a paper', 'write a thesis'. Not unless you have a constant level of superhuman motivation. Your goals need to be much more specific and achievable.

One example of a high level goal might be:

I will run a marathon in 6 months' time by training 5 days a week, covering a minimum of 30 miles a week

I would find this goal unachievable if that was all I had, despite it appearing to be a SMART goal. I would need sub goals below it per week and per day. I say this as someone who used to run half marathons. I would need a 'on week one of training I will run so many miles' and 'on day one of week one I will do X miles'. Otherwise, I would get to the end of week one supposedly needing to run 30 miles that week having run none and facing up to the fact that I would have failed at the first hurdle as there was no way I was running 30 miles on a single weekend. This kind of failure can really get into your head and change how you feel about the next stage and ensuring you don't make life harder for yourself is a key life lesson. Therefore, planning your SMART goals so each one runs at the right level for your needs is a key start to the goal setting process.

The purpose of a goal is that it should enable you to cut out the noise and focus on the now, not become a distraction or thing to be overcome. A good goal should enable you to be motivated even when you don't feel like it. A good goal should give you an objective way to capture progress, even when you feel you aren't making any. They should aid focus, rather than be something that makes life harder. You need to acknowledge that you will not feel world beating every day. What good looks like will change on different days and at different phases of your PhD. It is foolish, therefore, to pretend otherwise when you are planning your goals and sub goals. You need to be planning for reality, not idealism. It is not only sensible but essential therefore to include flexibility in your goal setting that takes this into account.

One of the best ways I've found to do this is to make sure that I have a mix of different styles and types of goals. I include tasks for those days where I don't have the focus for sustained deep activities, where all I can face is picking around the edges, as well as ones for those days when I can tackle the big thinking and can really dig deep. A good example of this is making sure you have a list of the essential, time consuming but slightly mindless work that always needs to be done for any paper or thesis. Things like figure checking, formatting wrinkles and cross referencing. Don't waste your days when you have energy and focus on these, keep a list to one side so that even on days you don't feel 'on it' you are able to still feel like you are moving things forwards. Be cognisant of your state of mind and use that to make the best use of your time.

Sometimes, seeing the big picture and doing high level thinking is what you need, and what you have the energy to achieve. There are other times, however, when seeing that big picture can feel overwhelming or dis-empowering, and what is needed is to be able to break any task/goal into small enough chunks to be able to just take the steps forward. In all honesty, those chunks have to be pretty damn small if I'm struggling. Occasionally, they can be larger, and they can be the focus of a whole day. Some days, the aim is at controlling the next 5 minutes of your life in order to keep moving forward.

In reflection of this, no goal stage should take longer than you can attain in one sitting. That one sitting could be a day, on some days that one sitting could be 20 minutes, but one sitting is my time boundary for setting an individual sub goal.

There are a few reasons for this:

- Different sub goals can get combined based on how you're feeling and your capacity to be challenged on any specific day
- Keeping them time limited means that they are easier to monitor, tick off and see progress, even when it feels like a slog
- It is easier to plan your total work that needs to be achieved/go into something if you have a workable unit of input that is going to be required
- It means that you only ever have to do one achievable thing in order to feel like you've done something.

All of this doesn't mean that you can't use goal setting to work towards a big plan, a big vision, or a big task. If you are working towards your 5-year plan, your thesis, your fellowship, you absolutely need to have a plan and goals that encompasses everything. The plan cannot however be 'write a thesis' or even 'write a thesis by the end of 2025'. Those types of goals are the ones that become millstones as they include all the expectation aspects of a goal with none of the pathway that would enable you to achieve what's needed.

Multistage goals require you to look at your big picture and then turn it into a 1000 piece jigsaw, where most of the time you are trying to find a home for a single piece, but you keep the lid of the box with the picture to hand in order to guide you along the way. Getting to a point where you are able to break the whole down requires you to do 2 things. One, do your research so you know about the project/larger goal in detail. This enables you to sensibly decide where you can segment it. Two, spend some time getting to know yourself, what motivates you and your rhythms, so that you can be sure you are breaking down the whole in a way that facilitates rather than hinders the way that you work. There is no point in being deluded and pretending you are or work like someone else. At this point, realism, no matter how much you like or dislike the truth, is key.

SMART goals also require that a good goal should be measurable. There are a couple of reasons for this. First, at a very basic level you need to be able to tell when it's been completed. Setting a goal like 'improve my piano skills' sounds fine, but how do you classify that? When will enough improvement be reached? Is sitting for 5 minutes and running scales enough, or are you wanting to be able to play more than Chopsticks?

Second, if you are involved in something that is big or multi goal, you will need to be able to see progress being made. Part of this, if you think like me, is that you need to be able to visualise that you're moving forward to maintain motivation. The other component of this is about learning for future activities. By setting measurable goals that have time scales attached, in order to capture trends, it supports you to be able to set better goals in the future. For instance, I know that I always under allocate time and have learnt the hard way that I need to add 1/4 additional time to things vs. the time I originally planned. I have also learnt that I will take an age on the initial phases of any piece of work, way longer than I had allocated. This means, however, that my writing phases tend to be much shorter than allocated, as if I've done my planning/thinking. You will have your own trends, but you need to learn what they look like for you.

The other thing to consider is that you will only get the full learning potential out of goals if you see those goals as live items. Pieces of a puzzle that should be regularly reviewed by holding them up against the box lid, which has the wider picture. Goals that are no longer helping should be reviewed, and the whole plan should remain flexible enough to change so that it can better fulfil the purpose. If you find out that you have allocated time scales that don't work, missed out crucial stages, or just made individual goals too big and need to break them up, this is much easier to fix if you embed reflection throughout. I would advocate setting reflection points at regular time intervals, but also at the start and end of a new stage, in order to think what went well and not so well.

For instance, if you are writing the first data chapter of your literature review, were your time allocations correct? How did your list of mop up activities work? Was there anything you missed out or had present that you didn't need? Then, use this learning to adjust everything moving forward. It's also worth having a wider review stage at the end so that you can roll any higher level themes into your learning for next time. You may not write another thesis, but you will write other large documents, so maximise the learning opportunities wherever possible.

At the end of the day, you, rather than the goal, are the one who needs to be in control. The purpose of all of this thinking and preparation is not, in the end, to make extra work for yourself. The purpose of this is to give yourself a framework to support thought and to ensure you don't waste time or lose direction later on. A goal is a tool to help, not a noose to choke self-confidence or creativity. The other thing to bear in mind is that a goal is not a deadline, and we should stop treating them as such. A goal is a way of helping you deliver to deadlines, but it is not an end in itself. You will have goals for things that don't have formal deadlines, and you may even have deadlines for things that don't require goals. Knowing the difference and seeing goal setting as just another tool in your toolkit that is there to help you achieve and reach your aspirations can really help change your relationship with goals and goal setting. If your goal does take control and end up becoming a deadline in itself, lay back and enjoy the feeling that comes with the sound of it whooshing past in order to re-set your relationship and put yourself back in the driving seat. You are the one in control after all.

Head to the Girlymicrobiologist website for a template that can help you do this.

CHAPTER ELEVEN: MANAGING DEADLINES AND MAKING ROOM FOR INSPIRATION

Speaking of your tool kit, there are plenty of things that will sit alongside goal setting that can help with the work of undertaking a PhD. Everyone enters a PhD at a different place. The same is also true for PhD projects, some are more developed on day one than others, especially if you have applied via the Fellowship route with a fully developed project proposal. It can be hard therefore to work out how you are doing. There are two things that can really help with navigating this, in addition to goal setting. The first is linked to knowing how to manage deadlines, which may or may not link into your goal setting. The second is managing the more creative and conceptual parts of the PhD process. Understanding how to find room for creativity, and then how to turn these ideas into concepts that can inform and be applied to your research.

The first of these tools is to learn how to know when a deadline is a deadline and when a deadline is more of a suggestion or window for submission. How to be aware of when your deadline is self-imposed, and linked to your goal setting, or whether it is a genuine deadline with an immovable schedule. For instance, projects will often have individual timelines, if they are grant funded, that you need to maintain. Grant funded projects will usually have milestones, reporting, and dissemination deadlines, which need to be kept to. Your goal related deadlines, as set up in the previous chapter, however, may be more self-imposed, and therefore may need to be considered differently.

Below are a few examples of different types of deadlines to be aware of and can help you understand the impact on your planning:

- True deadlines – papers for committee meetings, grant deadlines etc. This is where a number of subsequent actions are riding on yours and if you don't deliver, the domino effect is both real and important in the wider scheme of things
- Gate keeping deadlines – manuscript review deadlines for other authors, 1st draft deadlines for outlines, etc. This is where the task needs to happen, and in a timely fashion. The exact date itself, however, is arbitrary and so as long as communication is good and the time period doesn't

substantially extend, the process itself is unharmed

- Courtesy deadlines – submitting a conference presentation 3 days ahead (normally), arranging planning meetings etc. These often get given dates to ensure that they happen, but in reality, as long as they get done before they evolve into a true deadline i.e. before presenting at the conference, then the timescale is actually flexible

It is really important to understand what kind of deadline you're dealing with, otherwise you will treat everything as a true deadline which means that you may deliver on a courtesy deadline over a true deadline, with the associated consequences. Without understanding what type of deadline you have, you cannot really be aware of all of the possible options you can take when you are truly overwhelmed and unable to deliver on everything.

The other aspect of this is being aware of when the deadlines are for other people not for you. Courtesy deadlines are often there to make other people's lives or processes run more smoothly, and I would always support being a good colleague. That said if meeting a courtesy deadline means that you will incur a substantial personal cost, then this is a time to put your communication skills to the test and think about re-framing the deadline. You may also want to consider these deadlines differently based on who is issuing them. If they are coming from your supervisor in order to enable them to have time to review your work, they may sound like a courtesy deadline, but they are actually gate keeping deadlines. Ensure you take into account the relationship in your decision making, as well as the work itself.

Another side of this coin is, that as a PhD student, you will often be requiring others to keep to your deadlines, in order to move your work forward. This can include everything from needing others to order your consumables, to getting fellow authors to reply to your draft manuscript and having your supervisor review and return work you have submitted. You need to be clear with others about the type of deadline you are issuing and the impacts on you if not achieved. This is a key part of managing your supervisor and the rest of your PhD team. You cannot have everything that you are asking for to be treated as a true deadline, and you can only issue items as gate keeping deadlines that are. If you constantly pitch items incorrectly then everyone will downplay what you are asking. This means that your timelines will slip even more than they may do otherwise.

Once you know which deadlines are really deadlines and which are deadlines can be negotiated, for both yourself and others, you are then in a position to be able to prioritise. Now, this isn't just about juggling all those deadline balls, it's also about when you have to prioritise yourself. It's important to take ownership, it's important to be accountable, but not at the expense of your health and mental wellbeing. This can often be challenging, as working out where we are on the list of priorities is frequently hard to determine when you are in it. This is why checking in with others, and finding helpful critical friends, as well as using your supervision team, who can give context and perspective may help.

There are a number of tools that can be useful when managing both your own deadlines, or in keeping others to deadlines to help you keep to yours:

- Aim for clear communication to support prioritisation – be clear about the reason for the deadline, to aid prioritisation, as well as the timeline itself. Be clear that you will follow up with prompts or chasers at certain time points in the lead up to the deadline if it is a true deadline
- Share the load – use diary holds and calendar reminders in combination with emails to establish deadlines and deadline types and then follow up
- Utilise your calendar - clear diary time and include it as a specific hold to do that task, rather than just having it on a to do list. Manage this alongside your goal setting tools
- Clarify deadlines - ask about deadlines up front before you take on something and be prepared to negotiate your involvement. Is this something you have to do or is it that you want to be involved with? Can you meet their deadlines? Can you adjust their deadlines, so they work for you too?

The other process that you need to make space for, amongst all the deadlines and project plans, is for focusing on research questions and creating an environment that supports having ideas. This sounds like the simplest thing, but I think it's often an undisclosed struggle for many, and a source of silent pressure that might benefit from being acknowledged, especially when you're just starting out. PhDs are doctorates of philosophy for a reason, but it can sometimes be easy to get so caught up with the 'doing' that you don't make enough time for creative thought.

Academia, at its best, should be driven by ideas, questions, and developing concepts. All areas which require us to be able to ask new questions and sometimes see the world or challenges in a different way to those who've come before. This is at its heart linked to creative thought, and creativity is in itself is a process. It's something that requires the identification of time to allow ideas to be inspired, developed and reflected on. This is true whether you are a natural ideas person, who needs this time to be able to sort through too many thoughts to feel less overwhelmed, or someone who needs space to allow the ideas themselves for formulate.

Now, I'm not going to say good ideas because I believe you don't know whether an idea is good or bad until much further down the line, ideas aren't weighted at the start, they are just ideas. Sometimes, the most far out one's turn out to be best and sometimes the most solid appearing ones turn out to be a waste of time. Which brings me to thought number one: inspiration shouldn't involve a value judgement. Being open to ideas requires time and occasionally bravery, but the shifting process, where you consider whether an idea has legs, comes later.

Occasionally, the pressure to solve things or come up with ideas can feel a lot like writers' blocks. Staring at empty screens, lab books, or grant templates can lead to procrastination. Sometimes you need a kick-off point. I find reading (or going to listen to people speak) can often be helpful at this point. I'm not talking about reading for critique here but reading for inspiration. Academia is often a process driven environment, with a focus on outputs. If we are not 'doing research' time is considered to be wasted, but sometimes we need to read with a different purpose in mind. I think reading for inspiration is probably a different skill to reading for research. It's the opposite of trying to focus on the details like we normally do. It's reading and almost actively listening and recognising those little side tracking 'what if' thoughts that we would often try to ignore.

When reading for inspiration, you may also want to try different content that you would normally engage with. You might want to read about your subject from a different disciplines' perspective, for instance, infection control but from a human factors perspective. You might want to read about another use of a technique you use that isn't within your specialism. You may even want to read less formal articles, such as blog posts, to get a different perspective. The main thing is to be cognisant in your approach and be open to going down some mental rabbit holes to see where they lead.

Once you have your list of thoughts and have entered your inspiration phase, one of the things I try to encourage is finding a space to just let your mind wander, take a walk in the park, or stare at the rain through a window to free your mind. Counterintuitively, sometimes this is the most valuable time you will spend during your PhD. It can be hard to be passive however, I for one am not really good at just 'being'. If you are like me therefore you may decide a kitchen disco is the best way to free your mind or to go for a run instead. Find a way that allows you to distract your mind to enable you to see things in a different way, whatever way that works for you, is the main thing.

Once you've done with your inspiration phase the next step is deciding what to do with all those ideas. This requires some form of action, often doing some further reading or sitting down to grow that thought and specifically reflect and write about how that germ of an idea might grow into a more fully formed question or piece of work. This step is not always easy. There are some days where my mind is a hell to me, and I think if it was visualised, it would just be a cloud of buzzing flies. On days like this, I write. I write blog posts. I write post-it notes. I scribble notes in books. Writing things down, even if not directly to do with your research thoughts, creates a little space so that you can see the wood for the trees. It empties the mind on specific topics so you can gain clarity on other things and do the development work needed.

This is probably the time to hit the reading for research portion of development. This is the development part of the ideas phase. This is where you read more closely around the idea itself and start to see what others have done, undertake your gap analysis, and begin to think about the practicalities of undertaking the work. Because this question develop part can be painful it's something that you may procrastinate over. You may just want to sit in the lovely inspiration phase where all your thoughts are still possibilities. The truth of the matter is that it is easy to justify staying in the inspiration phase as it can be hard to know when you've done enough thinking and prep to move an idea to the next stage. However, if you never try moving from an idea to a reality you will also never succeed, and so sometimes we all need to pull off the psychological Band-Aid and just try it out.

To aid this transition make sure you have a structured way of recording your thought processes, and research questions, and that you keep them constantly updated with enough detail that you will understand them if you have to look at them in later years. Make sure you have everything written down and don't miss crucial details which were blatantly obvious at the time. I can promise you that when you come to look at them three years down the line you will have no idea what that obvious information was.

No matter where you are on your PhD journey, learn to trust yourself. Trust your instincts. Trust you will always have another idea. Trust that you will always be able to come up with a research plan B. Trust that there are people out there who will want to help and support. Then use both them and the tools available to you to support transitioning from an ideas phase to a research phase, where you are actually implementing your ideas. Utilise tools, like deadline setting, to help your progression, by setting deadlines for yourself and for others. Understand that while there always feels a gulf between the development of ideas and the making those ideas happen, the two are more connected than they may initially appear, and so you need to utilise tools to manage both in order to fully reach your potential.

CHAPTER TWELVE: MANAGING EXPECTATIONS

The first thing I want to talk about is setting your own expectations for your PhD. The reality of undertaking a PhD is that it can be incredibly challenging some days, but we all have to remember that our success at ticking actions off our list does not define who we are as people. I want to say this first therefore, before I go into anything else, and I want to say it loudly and on repeat – failed research does not make you a bad researcher. I shall say it again – failed research does not make you a bad researcher. All researchers fail, some of us have failed for months at a time, and challenging research is the name of the game. If you were doing something that had been done before, you wouldn't be doing PhD level work. Therefore, failure, far from being a flaw, is to be expected. The sooner this is accepted, the better your mental health will be.

Bearing that in mind, it's also worth remembering that PhD's are apprenticeships in research, and all of the failed research approaches or rabbit holes that don't pay off are far from a waste. They are part of the learning. You will use them to create your method development sections of your thesis, and they will give you great discussion points for your viva. In fact, if you had a completely clean sailing PhD that might be the more unexpected thing if I was your examiner, I'd be forced to dig more about where your learning happened.

Also, and I hate to do this as it's the tritest thing ever, but some of the best research comes from mistakes and screw ups. Think Fleming and penicillin. The main thing is the mind set through which we view the failure. If we take it personally and let it get in our heads, all we can see is failure. Some of my best science has happened when failure has made me take a step back and pause, and suddenly I've seen the problem in a new light, or it's forced me to make connections I wouldn't have normally thought about. Sometimes we need to be sure we see the failure as an opportunity rather than the end of hope.

Having got that out of the way, I also want to discuss the fact that although it can be soul destroying when something you've worked on for weeks or months crashes and burns, it can do more than act as part of the learning process. Research failures can also be a warning sign about the pace and intensity of your work and can, in the end, offer a useful way to self-check and force you to review your working patterns to provide a better and more sustainable pathway to success. If you are crying over a failed project, it's probably an indication that you need a break or to work differently.

This brings me onto the need to manage your expectations for your project itself. One of the biggest lessons I've learnt during my time working in science and doing research is that sometimes you have to be prepared to stop what you're doing. I've had to learn when to continue down the rabbit hole and when to pivot. During my PhD I spent 18 months trying to separate Adenovirus from Vero cells using centrifugation to reduce whole genome sequencing read loading towards monkey rather than viral DNA. You know what, I got a bit of a reduction, but not enough to make a real difference, and to get that I worked till midnight for months as that was the only time the ultra-centrifuge was available. What I didn't do was a) set some success criteria b) stick to them and c) have a cut off that was based on effort vs reward. I just carried on...and on…and on for very little payoff when I should have just stopped.

There will be times when you just need to persevere, as the work you are doing is central to the project and definitely achievable. Anything core should be designed at the project level as attainable. There will, however, always be other aspects that need to be evaluated for the resource they are requiring (time, money, etc) vs what they are adding to your body of work. There is no point in spending 18 months on something that will be 2 pages in your thesis, there is point in spending 12 months fixing something that will be a chapter or more.

A key skill to develop is the ability to step back and see where the piece you're currently working on fits into the whole and then evaluate what level of effort it is worth. If you haven't set your success criteria etc beforehand it can be super painful to reach this decision and to walk away. This can be why having a good project timeline for your work/project/PhD can be really helpful. It helps you make pragmatic decisions and gets you out of the weeds in order to help you move forward with a view of the work as a whole.

One of the things that can with the 'rabbit hole or pivot' conundrum is getting to know yourself enough to understand when you are in a spiral. When you are becoming obsessive about succeeding, and too deep into the issue, rather than being able to step away and see the whole. Your willpower and persistence are probably the big reasons why starting a PhD is the right route for you. The downside to these aspects of academic personalities is that you can become hyper focused on a goal and the fact that it has to happen. You can get in your own way when this happens and lose the ability to do the required reflection piece. The end result of this is that it takes you longer than it should to realise you should have stopped and re-focussed your attentions on an alternate approach.

This is where making sure you have regular access to your supervisor and using them to discuss your project, can definitely help managing your PhD. Discussions with your supervisor can assist in making sure you always have a plan B, and ideally C and D. Research will always be filled with highs and lows. It will always ebb and flow. There's no escaping this fact. What I have learnt though is there are routes to being savvier about anticipating these peaks and troughs. I had a fairly horrid experience during one of my master's degrees, where the project was designed as just one thing that either worked or it didn't. Inevitably it didn't, and I was forced to write 10,000 words on 3 results. This taught me 2 valuable lessons, 1) never blindly follow a project designed by someone else, if you feel it isn't right for you, own the fact that it is your project and you need to input to get it where it needs to be, and 2) never design a project that is entirely dependent on plan A working, as the chances are it won't.

Taking a modular approach to any project design, when working on your project plan, will enable you to combine parts that work and still have an overarching narrative that makes sense and that enables you to succeed, even if individual components fail. If you are designing a project around a core component that you are then attaching spokes to, that core component needs to be guaranteed in terms of process success, even if not result outcomes, as you can discuss the results in the context of your work, but you can't risk not being able to get them. Take time to map this out and to undertake a SWOT (strengths, weaknesses, opportunities and threats) analysis, so you can pre-plan for how you will manage any failures. That way you won't lose time panicking when things go wrong as you will have a defined pathway already.

This brings me onto managing the expectations of others, especially those of your supervisor. All the tools we've discussed, from learning agreements to goals/project plans and SWOT analysis, are essential tools for you to be able to better describe where you are aiming for, where you are currently at, and the barriers or challenges you are facing. Bringing all of those data points to your discussions with your supervisory team, can mean that, not only are you helping them help you, but also that you are being clear about how you are doing so that they can set and adjust their expectations appropriately. Some of the biggest challenges with supervision occurs when you don't communicate effectively and therefore one, or both sides, believes they are in a different position to the one that is the reality. This leads to frustration, and also potentially increased risk of failure, as all of the actions needed to mitigate those risks aren't being undertaken. Providing concrete data on positioning can help avoid this very real pitfall.

The final expectation that you will want to consider managing is that linked to your friends and family, especially if they don't have experience of the PhD journey. This is a project that will go on for years, but from the outside many people expect it to be similar to the experience of undertaking undergraduate study. They often don't realise how complex and challenging a progression it actually is. This means that you may find a lot of people asking 'when are you going to submit?' or 'aren't you done yet?' after only a year or so. My advice is to sit down with your key supports, be they family or friends, and talk them through what the process of taking a PhD is like and be clear about the kind of support you might need. You may even want to give them a copy of this book, so they will understand your journey better. You want your friends and family to be the source of support you need, not another source of unwarranted expectation or pressure. It is hard to truly convey both the highs and lows of undertaking a PhD. The extreme satisfaction when it goes well, or how lonely it can be when you are struggling, but if you start those conversations early on you will be better placed to get the support you need.

Managing expectations is not about extremes, it is not about assuming that everything is always going to go well or bemoaning the fact that nothing will ever go right. It's about identifying the strengths and weaknesses of your approach, both for the project, but also for your PhD as a whole and using that awareness to support your planning to aid future success. All research will have good points, as well as items that need to be considered as they could cause issues if you don't address them. Being aware of this yourself is important, but it's also crucial to involve your supervisory team in the discussion so they can help stave off some of the issues and elevate some of the opportunities. Take time to make sure everyone is sighted, to ensure that you get all the support you need to minimise your stress and maximise your potential. Linking this in with your goal setting, and project management, will give you the best possible start to the first year of your PhD.

Head to the Girlymicrobiologist website for a template that can help you do this.

CHAPTER THIRTEEN: IDENTIFYING PEER SUPPORT

Academia is far more than undertaking research. Did you sign up and deliver some kick ass outreach? Did you ask a great question in a group meeting? Did you make your struggling peer a cup of tea or help them with a figure they couldn't get right? All of these are key activities to aid in developing as an academic, but also in establishing your networks. Frankly, you can't be an academic alone, that's why I really believe that research is a team sport. Sometimes, you will need someone else to help you recognise that it's time to evaluate. Sometimes, you will need the support of others as part of the reflection process, and when it comes to troubleshooting why things are not working. Two heads are definitely better than one. You will always have your supervisor to help with this, but peers, whether part of the academic world or not, can offer a very different type of benchmarking and support to that provided by your supervision team. Identifying these people early and developing your relationships and building trust will pay dividends throughout your PhD experience. So, find them early for maximum benefit.

The start of any PhD is about not just starting your academic career journey, but about becoming acquainted, and embedded, in a world of new cultural norms. Becoming part of the academic world at this level is so different from being part of it as an undergraduate or course-based post graduate student. I've talked about a PhD being a job, and this is definitely true in this aspect. There's a lot of understanding how things work. Who will order your pens? How do you log onto courses? Do you have to book out desk space? How will conference travel work? How does the IT system work? Where can you make tea? Where can you send your posters for printing? There will be so many questions and things to learn. Your supervisor is not going to be the person that helps you with most of these details. There is likely to be administrative support, but who does what? Getting to know other PhD students or post docs will enable you to have someone to speak to and ask questions as they come up, which will be invaluable so that you don't lose time or make mistakes.

Fellow students can also help signpost opportunities or experiences that your supervisors may be less aware of. Are there good discounts that may make your life easier? Where do you register for cards that will give you student discounts? Are there book exchanges or special interest groups that can help you either academically or creating a new social circle? Even something as simple as which lunchtime meetings provide food can really help your stipend stretch that little bit further. When you are trying to tackle so much at the start, it can be easy to not really focus on this more social aspect of starting out, but you will be living in this world for a minimum of three years, and therefore you need to recognise that social and soft skills will be as necessary to your success as your academic progression.

One of the big reasons to develop peer support is that, even if you have a great relationship with your supervisor, even if everything is going well, there will be times when you dislike them or parts of your PhD. This is both natural and OK. When these times hit, however, you will need to have safe spaces to vent and seek support. Speaking to your peers can enable you to practice conversations you want to have with your supervisor, in order to increase confidence and help with your thinking. It's important, therefore, to invest time early on to build wider relationships with your peers, as it will take time to get to know people well enough to know who you would be happy to have these conversations with. Everyone is different and therefore not everyone who counts as a peer is someone you would want to approach for support. This is especially true if you are working in a smaller group. You may, therefore, need to seek out additional groups or networks in order to access sufficient peer support and find people that work for you. These contacts will stand you in good stead during your PhD, but also in your future career, as learning to build networks is a key skill to be invested in. Far from being a sign of weakness, seeking support and building networks so you have identified that support are key parts of your career development.

Listening informally to conversations, making time to go to the pub or for lunch or coffee, to hear other members of your peer group talk about how they are feeling, their goals and ambitions, and issues, will help with understanding where you are and what your drivers are. Checking in with yourself about how you respond to some of the statements made can be helpful as your reactions may aid your reflections on what you find important. Listening to the challenges that others are facing can also help you prepare for the challenges that are likely to crop up for you in the future. This can be helpful as by aiding someone else through their blocks will mean that you are learning strategies if approaching them yourself in case you ever face a similar situation. It can help so you don't just replicate the mistakes of others and so time spent in this setting is just good resource management.

Another reason why it might be helpful to develop academic peer support, is to aid in benchmarking. We've talked a little about goal setting and managing expectations, both processes which can be aided by inclusion of discussion with peers. It can help with your reflection processes to talk about your thinking linked to project planning and timelines. One word of warning on this one. It is not always meaningful to benchmark against your peers, as PhDs by their very nature need to be unique pieces of work, so someone can appear to be killing it, but their track record will look different to yours as will the challenges they face in the future. I would always, therefore, advocate for using peer benchmarking as a source of support rather than self-judgement, as you may not be comparing like with like.

Having talked about why peer support is important, how do you develop it, especially if you are far from home and your normal friendship groups? Getting out and attending group meetings, or other teaching, can be a great way to not only meet people but also to develop the subject specific language you'll need to succeed. If, like I was, you are part of a much smaller group, or even the only PhD student in your department, then your funders may be able to signpost you to other people on similar schemes. You should have access to a postgraduate tutor who will be able to tell you about postgraduate welcome events, committees, or other meetings that will enable you to make connections across departments/buildings. Social media can also be your friend, as there are a number of good university or university associated social media accounts that can be a valuable source of information. There should also be groups or links with professional societies, or subject specific groups, that are worth investigating and joining. These will give you access to external meetings, events, and often funding sources, and so despite requiring a small financial outlay, are often a great investment.

One final way to find peers that might work for you is to engage in activities that support not only your academic skill development but also allow you to work with people you might not have engaged with otherwise. This can include things like volunteering for open days, joining outreach schemes, or even putting yourself forward to sit on committees, such as early career committees or equality, diversity and inclusion committees. It can also include things in your department, like volunteering to help organise journal clubs, regular teaching, or tea rotas. These activities enable you to be proactive in developing skill sets or gaining experience, but will also mean that you get to work closely with people you might not encounter in your day to day work. As these are opt in activities, you may also be more likely to find people that align with your interests as you have chosen these options as they work for your individual aspirations and learning needs.

Finding the right people and surrounding yourself with them during your PhD can make so much difference to your experience, and your chances of success, both during and afterwards. You need the people that will help you through your academic thinking, the people that you can have conversations with to help guide and benchmark you, but you also need the people that you can relax with, moan with and celebrate with. The earlier you find them, the better, so you should do so with purpose and make time. This one is both an investment in your PhD, but also in yourself and your wellbeing.

CHAPTER FOURTEEN: MARKING YOUR SUCCESSES

Projects that go on for years, such as your PhD, will always have ups and downs. Moments of challenge, and moments of success. They will contain a lot of firsts. Your first paper (hopefully). Your first conference presentation. The first journal club you lead. Your first presentation to your group. Your upgrade, and eventually your thesis submission and viva. It can feel tempting to focus on the final sentence in that list and let the other moments pass you by, but in the terms of your academic career, all of them are big moments that should be marked and savoured, at least for a while.

The challenge comes in deciding whether the event is 'sufficient' and worthy of celebration. It can be easy, at least work wise, to be so focused on an end goal or big picture that nothing is considered to be worthy of celebration along the way. The problem with this is that there is always another step, another target, and so if celebration is not prioritised, it may just never happen. Success and reasons to celebrate come in all shapes and sizes. It is easy to get into the habit of needing external validation, prizes and the like, in order to measure how well you're doing or to feel worthy of celebration. These are lovely, but there are some problems with using this as a yardstick.

Firstly, how many prizes and awards can you realistically actually win across your career, and are you suddenly worthless when they become unavailable? The other issue is that if we need others to tell us our value, rather than being able to see it in ourselves, you are constantly in a vulnerable position, especially with people who would use that requirement against you. It is a necessary step in growth to be able to see that we have intrinsic value and to celebrate that, rather than relying on others to see our worth. My plea on this one is that we all take time to celebrate the little things as well as the big things. Sometimes in life, merely getting out of bed is worth a celebratory cup of tea. This is why understanding your goals and setting appropriate rewards is so important.

But why should celebration be prioritised anyway? One of the key reasons is that it is easy to forget how far you've come and to not sufficiently recognise your true progress if individual moments are not recognised. Ensuring that you take the time to celebrate is a key part of you recognising your progress and investing in some self-care. Once you have 50 published papers, it's easy to forget what having the first one accepted felt like. Once you have passed your upgrade, it is easy to downplay how insurmountable it felt at the start. Celebrating can help ensure that you remember that feeling, which is important when you move on to supervision, but also ensures you recognise that you have achieved the thing that once felt out of reach.

It's important to also know that success feels different at different moments in life. There have certainly been times where the successes I've marked have not been about the big things. They haven't been about winning large amounts of grant funding or awards. My successes have been about getting through the week, and to be honest, sometimes they have been about getting through the day. A PhD is a challenging thing and sometimes it is at these moments that we have to note the successes that we do have even more. At these times, for me, it's about finding and celebrating the small wins and setting myself small targets, in order to feel like I'm still moving forward.

Self-awareness in these moments is key. Be aware though that not everything is worthy of a reward. In my world, I still have to set and meet a target. It's just that target gets flexed based on the reality I find myself in. I still have to do the work; there is no free pass. You consciously adjust your goals to reflect the fact that more structure will aid in keeping you moving forward, but also acknowledge the effort required to gain that progress and build yourself in something that marks that effort. For instance, when I was training for my first half marathon, and as part of my training ran my first 5K race and finished, I allowed myself to buy myself a dress I'd wanted for ages. It doesn't have to be a big thing; it can be buying your favourite chocolate bar. It can be taking a break and watching an episode of your favourite TV programme. It just has to be something that is celebratory for you. You can celebrate and have the reward for small things, but it must still be earned to have meaning.

Recognising individual stages of progress can also help with the big stages. Sometimes, completing a task, such as writing a PhD thesis, can just seem unattainable. Breaking down the massive task into sections that feel more achievable and allowing yourself to recognise that progress can, mean the entire task feels more manageable. It can also help maintain momentum and positive attitude during tasks that are particularly challenging or where it can be easy to become bogged down. After all, most of the learning, and therefore the reason to celebrate, occurs as part of the journey rather than just at the destination.

Traditionally, success is often seen as moving from point A to point B. In reality, success is more like a series of concentric circles where improvement is cumulative and often based on iterative improvement. Therefore, any journey actually has a lot of near misses with success before success occurs. It's important to notice when these near misses occur, rather than just discounting them as failures. Celebrate your first draft, as well as your final submission, even if that submission isn't initially successful. Celebrate the submission, as well as the final acceptance. Take a moment out to reflect on and celebrate the learning that has happened, and progress made, without having to acquire someone else's permission by earning approval or ticking a box in order to have permission to do so.

Another thing to bear in mind is that celebrations are not just about you. They are an opportunity for you to give back and acknowledge the input and impact of others. By choosing not to celebrate, we also steal an opportunity away that could be used to thank and recognise colleagues, friends, and family, without whom none of this stuff would happen. Not just that though. By celebrating successes, you not only share the success and say thank you to those who have helped, but you are also visible to others and show that those attainments are possible. This can make real difference to your peers, and other people who are currently facing challenge along their academic journey. By sharing your successes and being visible, you will also be inspiring others, so don't be afraid to be seen.

Having spoken earlier about not relying too much on external validation, that doesn't mean that you should not engage with it at all. External validation can be great; it's just not something that can always be relied upon to be consistently accessible and so shouldn't be the only way. Sharing and celebrating the work of yourself and others can be aided by nominating for these external markers of success. I'm talking here about nominations for awards or prizes to recognise both yourself and your peers. Many professional societies, as well as universities, will have annual prizes or award categories. These will almost always accept self-nominations as well as nomination of others. It can feel odd to self-nominate, but as long as you nominate others to at least the same amount as you nominate yourself, then I think self-nominations are fine. Not least because it can be hard for someone else to know enough detail about your work to spontaneously nominate you. Even if your nominations of others are not successful, it can make a real difference to how they see themselves and their work, as someone else has taken the time to recognise it. Nomination writing is also a useful skill to develop, as it aids you to learn how to write to judging criteria and pitch. These are skills that are useful throughout your academic career, but you are learning them by doing something to aid in the visibility of everyone included.

You will encounter people who will try to mute your celebrations, who attempt to steal your joy. The thing is, that aspect will always be there, whether you celebrate or not. Whether you talk about it or not. The comments from others and people who don't understand what you are trying to achieve don't go away. You do, however, have the power to decide how much they influence your decision-making. To decide how much power they have over you. How much right they have to stop the work you are doing or to dampen all the reasons that you should celebrate and be seen to do so. You can't control the reactions of others, but you can control how they affect you. Aim to be inclusive in your celebrations, and clear about being open to the learning that got you to this place. The reactions of others are then theirs to worry about, not yours to be concerned with.

Finally, celebration is not just about you. To really embrace the art of celebration, we need to see it as the gift it is. We need to amplify the celebration of others! When you hear of good things happening, buy that card or bottle of fizz to support the person who may be struggling to feel they can celebrate. When you see a social media post, share it and comment on it. Let the person know how happy you are for them and help to get the word out. Be genuinely happy, rather than challenged, by the success you see all around you. People are showing you what can be achieved, and you are inspiring others. Let's aspire to be a community that values and celebrates success, not just our own but of everyone.

CHAPTER FIFTEEN: MAINTAINING YOUR WORK LIFE BALANCE

It is often discussed that PhDs are not 9 – 5 Monday to Friday. This is both true and not entirely the whole picture. There will be times when you have to pull long hours and weekends. There should also be times when you leave at midday on a Friday for a long weekend in order to take a proper break. It is also worth noting that for a PhD, work may not just be about sitting in front of your research or your computer. Work can also be walking through the park and thinking through a particularly challenging issue. When thinking about your work life balance during a PhD it's worth considering two things. First, think about when you are actually working and making sure you identify the whole spectrum of what that is, be it in front of a computer or not. Secondly, make sure you are intentional about when you are working and when you are not working, and don't blur the edges between the two. Work life balance is a difficult thing to identify sometimes, let alone to achieve. Start your PhD with a plan about how to flex based around the demands so you can achieve some form of it throughout your project.

Counterintuitively, let's start not with the life part of this chapter, but with the work part. Let's start by thinking of the things that get you out of bed in the morning. The things that drove you to start a PhD in the first place. The items that give you joy when you are in the workspace, no matter how hard your project is currently feeling. For me, this was always finally getting some time in the lab when no one else was around. Time to really get my teeth into the problem and crucially doing so with some cracking tunes playing in the background. Music that is playing far too loudly and allows me to joyfully fully engage with the science that I love. Everyone will enjoy different things, but making a list of those drivers, and activities that you can undertake alongside your other work, can help ensure that you integrate enough of them to ensure that you have some joy in your working day. I would start this process by making a list of all of the different activities that you undertake during an average week, or even month. Then start to categorise the list into things that you enjoy, tasks you are happy enough to get on with, and jobs you will actively avoid if given the option. Once you have this list you can then start to use it in your planning activities.

We've talked about the importance of goal setting and project planning. What we haven't talked about is also planning your work time to include a mixture of the activities on your list to bring some light and shade into your every day. If you are planning your literature review, and therefore will be writing for hours every day, you will need to plan some activities that enable you to do something else to break up your time. You will not be able to write for 8 hours a day, every day for three months. You will want to add in time for reading, time for walking and reflection. Crucially, if you don't really enjoy writing, you will want to plan in work rewards, where you break up your days with a different type of work activity that you do enjoy, both to aid productivity, but also to reward yourself. Using your list of different activity types by preference means that you can bring an extra dimension to your planning to ensure that you structure in a way that works best for you and your brain, whilst ensuring not all of it will be a hard slog.

This brings me onto planning the life part of your work life balance. It's not just in our working life that we have things that refresh us and things which drain us. Very rarely, however, do we spend time reflecting on the kinds of things we enjoy doing. The things that help us refresh our batteries. The things that mean, even if life is challenging, they enable us to come back and fight another day. So often in life we just 'do' things. We respond to invites, we buy tickets, we pick up books and take bubble baths. Starting out on a PhD though is a time to give more thought to these components of life that you take for granted, as they are likely to be times during your project where ensuring you have enough access to these things will require a little bit more planning. Being aware of what down time activities you truly value, versus those ones that you enact because of social obligations, is time that is well worth spending.

When doing this reflection, you want to consider a few different things. The first is, think about the type of activity when you are making your list of things that bring you joy. There are different types of activity that are helpful over the course of your PhD. You will want to consider things that are physical or keep you moving. This doesn't necessarily need to be the gym or exercising, it can be dancing, walking in the countryside, or DIY. The main thing is that it should involve being up and not sitting. This is because when you are facing times when you are doing a lot of sitting without moving for your work, you probably need to be finding a way to move and potentially get outside, to provide contrast. This will benefit your mental, as well as physical health.

The next thing you will want to consider is the kind of fully engaging cognitive activities you enjoy. If you are doing a lot of writing or making lots of notes you will have phases when you want a completely different type of intellectual activity to shift your brain into a different gear. This could be going to the theatre, watching movies, engaging with your favourite trashy TV. It can also be things like playing video games, or baking. Anything that requires a lot of your attention, but is also not too taxing, in order to be able to rest the part of your brain that is being worked a lot during your current work phase.

Finally, I would have a list of items that you find distract you and therefore can provide a complete break. This can be going for drinks with friends, meeting up with your family for lunch. It can be undertaking creative endeavours, such as painting or pottery. The type of activity that allows you to fully focus on something completely different from work, in order to allow you to completely step away and fully rest and recover.

The thing to bear in mind with any of your personal ways of re-energising and decompressing, is how many of them you are undertaking with your work colleagues or peers. We've talked about how important peer support is to your PhD journey, but it is worth bearing in mind that you will never be able to fully step away if the activity you're undertaking is with those same peers. You will inevitably end up talking about work, or some of your project challenges. That kind of conversation is important but cannot be considered as truly part of your re-energising activities. Make sure you maintain enough contact with the outside 'real' world, as if you only spend downtime with others in your PhD space you will never truly walk away from it.

This brings me onto boundaries. When entering any new phase of your life it is really important to consider your boundaries, and I would encourage you to include those boundaries as part of your learning agreement, as and when appropriate. These require some consideration, for instance, are you happy to connect with your peers on social media? Are you happy to be in a work WhatsApp where you may receive work related messages on the weekend? Do you only wish to be contacted by your supervisor by email, which you can choose as and when to access, or are you happy that they contact you via your phone or other means outside of emergencies?

You should also decide what boundaries you will set for yourself. Will you look at work emails on the weekend? Will you only do so when there is a Monday deadline? Will you set limits for yourself, where you only work one weekend a month? Or are you happy to work weekends as long as you leave work at 5pm every weekday? How firm are you going to be with yourself linked to lunch and other breaks? Are you happy to go to lunch time talks? I advise these as they are valuable, but will you only attend three times a week? Will you arrive every day before nine? Will you work on site every weekday? These boundaries are especially important if you have any caring responsibilities or health issues. Make sure you develop pragmatic boundaries and ensure that you have a way to monitor your adherence in order to help you stick to them. Also, bear in mind there may be periods where your self-imposed boundaries have to flex in response to your project plan or other PhD requirements. Be open about these boundaries, consider including examples such as working hours in email signatures etc, and ensure that you discuss them with your supervisor. If you struggle with setting boundaries yourself, make sure you find someone who can support you, a trusted friend or peer who can help.

Once you have got your list and established your boundaries, make sure that you include these in your project plan. Look at what kind of work you are undertaking and plan your downtime activities in a way that will support the best possible relaxation to counter what you have going on. This will also include being realistic with how much down time you are actually going to get. There is no point planning for entire weekends off if you know you have a major deadline coming up and not enough time to prepare if you just use your standard working hours. If you are entering a phase when downtime is tight, choose activities that are easy to include and embed. I will often download and include some downtime TV watching on my commute home, so I've already begun the wind down. Can you combine wind down activities, such as a bath and a good book, in order to maximise their effectiveness? Use the reflection you've undertaken on clustering activities to plan the best ones in combination with your work in order to help you achieving the best possible work life balance.

The last thing to think about in this section is being aware of how you react to stress and how this can impact your planning. Some people, when they are stressed, ostrich and just can't face the scale of the task ahead. This can lead to prevarication and hiding from the issue. Others just ramp up and up the hours worked, whilst becoming less and less efficient. Understanding how you respond to stress and monitoring how your work and relaxation plans are useful in order to self-monitor. If you suddenly track that you are working far under or far over the hours you had planned this either means your goal setting is off, or you may be behaving outside of your normal boundaries in response to stress. This can give you an early warning sign to address the source of that stress and think about re-planning your approach. None of us are machines, make sure you allow for the human factor in your responses and treat yourself with kindness.

Head to the Girlymicrobiologist website for a template that can help you do this.

TOP TIPS FOR SUCCEEDING IN YOUR FIRST YEAR

Hi, I'm Helen, one of Elaine's previous PhD students. She asked me to share some top tips I wish I'd known when I started out. I wanted to focus on the first year, because in many ways it's the most important year of your PhD. This is your chance to push yourself out of your comfort zone, try new things, make new friends, make mistakes, and say yes to opportunities. The foundations you lay now will support you throughout the rest of your PhD. Here are my top tips:

Build good habits early

Your first year is the perfect time to set up the routines that will carry you through the next three or four years. Find out what working patterns suit you best, whether that's doing lab work in the morning and writing in the evening, and take advantage of the flexibility a PhD offers. Elaine has covered aspects such as developing good relationships with your supervisor and getting into healthy work life balance routines, so I won't repeat these, but it is so much easier to stick to the routines and habits you have already developed when the going gets a bit tougher later down the line.

Start organising early

Building on this, future you will thank you for developing good organisational systems and strategies early on.

- Referencing: Pick a reference manager, and even if you don't properly insert the reference in each draft at least note down the author and year.
- Backups: develop a good system for saving documents so you can find them again and tell which on one the most current version, also please please get an external hard drive and back everything up once a month.
- Lab books: write down methods every time, in 3 years time you won't remember exactly which concentration of antibiotic you used.
- Meeting notes: Keep them all in one notebook or digital folder so they're easy to find later.

Say yes to as much as you can

The first year is a great time to explore and get involved. Say yes to:

- Attending talks and seminars, even if they're only loosely related to your project.
- Helping more experienced lab members or trying out a small side project, you'll learn skills that may be invaluable later.
- Joining departmental student activities and socials, building a support network will help during the harder times.

Plan your breaks (and actually take them)

It's very easy to keep delaying time off because there's always "just one more experiment." I found it really helpful to pre-book holidays or breaks, ideally with other people or some other form of commitment, so I couldn't talk myself out of them. Having breaks planned in advance helped me pace myself, recharge properly, and get a little bit of space and perspective away from the lab.

Get to know your new environment

If you've moved cities (or countries), make the most of it. Explore the area and the institution.

Make the most of your upgrade

The upgrade can feel daunting, but it's a valuable chance to step back, reflect, and get feedback from fresh eyes. The discussions I had with my examiners shaped my project in unexpected but positive ways. And the literature review I wrote for my upgrade report ended up being a big part of my final thesis.

Keep every draft

Never delete old versions of your work. Save them as new files. You'll find yourself writing about the same topics for different audiences, and sometimes an earlier draft has exactly the phrasing or explanation you need.

Ask for help if you need it

Don't be afraid to ask questions, no one expects you to know everything, particularly in your first year. Lean on your supervisors, lab mates, or other students. People are usually happy to share advice and experience. On the other hand, try not to worry about making mistakes, as long as it's not too expensive or dangerous then making mistakes is often the best way to learn and shape your project, and it matters a lot less in your first year.

Remember: you are more than your PhD

This journey will be a big part of your life over the next few years, but it doesn't define you. People like you for your kindness, humour, and personality, not because you know a lot about one niche subject.

Enjoy it!

Dr Helen Rickard - 2025

YEAR TWO

CHAPTER SIXTEEN: PREPARING YOUR UPGRADE/LITERATURE REVIEW

The first thing to say is congratulations on reaching the second year of your PhD! The first year of your PhD will have been all about orientating yourself and learning to plan for future success. The second year of your PhD is where that work really starts to crystalise into outputs, be that confirming your progress in an upgrade, attending your first conferences where you present work, or getting started on your first paper. I'm writing this as if these things will all happen in your second year, as that is often the case, but as I talked about a lot in year one, things happen at different times for different people. Each PhD is individual, and each discipline is different, so timelines do vary. Don't worry if some of these happen slightly later for you. If they happen even earlier, good job, but there's still a lot of consolidation and learning to be done, so use the fact that you will have more time to build on this foundation to get even better.

It is common in PhD programmes to have gateways, points at which your progress is evaluated to check that everything is going well, and your work is on track. These can happen at any time but there is often a larger evaluation that occurs somewhere around the middle to end point of your second year. What this looks like varies widely between countries, between universities, and departments. This evaluation can feel intimidating, but it is worth bearing in mind that it is not just you that is being evaluated, it is also the project itself and your supervision. Trust me, it's often pretty intimidating for your supervisors too.

Within UK PhDs, and some countries in Europe, you often register on a master's programme when you initially start, such an MPhil. You then undertake a process known as upgrading. This is a gateway where you undertake an assessment with someone external to your project. If you pass your upgrade, you can change your registration onto a DPhil for the rest of your studies. Not every university or programme does this. In the US, for instance, you may be registered on a formal master programme first or need to complete a certain number of master level credits at the start of your programme, which will involve their own assessments. You would then have a requirement to pass these in order to move to the next phase of your PhD.

Everyone undertaking a PhD, irrespective of topic, will have a period when you really start to review all the literature, so that you have the groundwork you need for your own work to build on that of others who've gone before. The output of this literature review is therefore one of the common ways that this evaluation is undertaken. Evaluation often requires a written submission, with or without a viva, in order to have an output that can be evaluated by someone external to the project. The review of the literature that you will have undertaken in year one into year two is therefore a common component that forms the basis for any examination submission.

By the time you come to write up you will have sat and read, probably thousands of papers, and now you are faced with having somewhere in the region of 10 – 15,000 words, in which to pull all of that together, and ideally include something about where your project sits and what you are trying to achieve. The critical challenge therefore is how do you get from an enormous pile of other people's work to a document that covers the salient points but supports your project?

A common approach is that students will just sit down and start to write sections that they think will be useful or interesting. I always discourage this approach. If you start by just writing without a plan, you will end up writing thousands of words that you either decide to ditch later, and have thus wasted time, or end up with a bloated unfocussed document that is really challenging for your examiner to assess. This process also tends not to result in what this process at it's heart is meant to achieve. This process is supposed to help you have an opportunity to really understand what your project is. What it is in the landscape of other literature. What it is in terms of your creative thought in pinning down what interests you and what you would like to explore further. All of which is aimed at supporting you to plan, in detail, the work of your PhD to get you through to preparing your thesis. If you miss the opportunity this gives you to do that thinking, develop that framework and make that plan, it will make the rest of your PhD that much harder.

Writing documents like this one benefit from your taking a very structural approach, one that is also good practice for your final PhD thesis as well. The first thing therefore is to spend a lot of time on some of the shortest pieces of text that you will eventually write, your hypothesis, aims and objectives. In your final document these will probably be less than one page, but every single word matters, and so getting this right is so important. Being able to be very descriptive in a limited number of words is a skill and you will probably end up with more versions of these than any other pieces of writing you do, in order to get it right. If you are fortunate, you may have some of this already done, either from grant or fellowship funding. Even those words will have been written prior to the in-depth work that has been undertaken as part of your literature review however, and therefore it will be necessary to revisit them. The process of revising these will be important to shaping your thinking for the entire of the rest of the document, and work closely with supervisors to make sure you maintain a shared vision of where your work is going.

The reason that getting your hypothesis, aims and objectives right is so important is that those will be used to shape the story that you want to tell using the literature, and your data if you have any to share. We'll talk more about telling a story with your work in the later chapters that focus on papers and your thesis, but the way to ensure that an examiner understands why your work is interesting, has value, and meets the PhD criteria, is about being clear about the story you are telling with your research. Stories have a beginning, a middle and an end, and presenting your work is no different. Your hypothesis, aims and objectives, provide the framework that you can then use to hang all of the other content on, so that it makes sense to the person reading it. These documents are not about showing the amount of reading you have done and referring to everything that has ever been published. As a researcher, a key skill is being able to access information, synthesise it, and then utilise it in concert with your knowledge to make something new. It's not about regurgitation. This gateway is a great way to be able to demonstrate that you have this skill set by showing you can identify significant pieces of work and understand how they impact your project.

Once you have your overarching story structured in your mind you can the start the structural drafting of your document. This starts by identifying which topic areas are needed to support the project that you are working on.

For instance, in my world, if I had a project title such as:

'Evaluating the use of genotypic techniques to investigate the genetic diversity, virulence, and antimicrobial resistance profiles of Klebsiella pneumoniae within paediatric healthcare settings'

I would know that I would need sections within my review on:

- Genotypic techniques
- Genetics of Klebsiella pneumoniae
- Klebsiella pneumoniae virulence factors
- Klebsiella pneumoniae antimicrobial resistance mechanism
- Antibiotics
- Healthcare and healthcare associated infections
- Klebsiella pneumoniae infections
- Children and paediatric healthcare

I would also need something about gold standards, as I have used the word evaluation in the title, therefore I have to be able to talk about how that evaluation or benchmarking will be undertaken. Everything is led from what I have already developed.

Every section should have a purpose and should work to support you communicating your work in a clear and concise way, whilst supporting the depth you need to communicate the literature. If you have too many sections, you end up being superficial in your discussions because you don't have the word count to support a deep dive into the research. You also want to decide on your sections in a systematic way, based on your aims, objectives, etc, as you don't want to miss a key section that is needed to support your work. Mapping your structure allows you to see that you have sufficient coverage, without including sections that take up word count and aren't additive.

This is another key moment to get supervisor input. It's common that students want to be able to show something that is really developed or nearing perfection. This can be really challenging. It's not that getting a document that is nearly finished isn't great to read, the problem is that it can be harder to see the structure behind it, so it can be more challenging to identify what is not quite right if changes need to be made. It can also mean that it leads to wasting a lot of writing time if your supervisor then comes back with substantial changes. If you submit your outline, you can work on it together with your supervisor and get input to check that the story that is clear in your mind is coming over the same way on paper. It is much easier to move headers and sections around to support flow when it is a series of headers and bullet points, rather than full sections of text that will need linkage paragraph edits and sometimes more. By spending time on getting this structuring right, you will save time as you should have less editing required when you have added in all of your text.

Once you have got all of your structure down it is time to then focus on the writing itself. My big suggestion here is to make sure that you have already identified and are using reference management software. I didn't do this until my thesis, and it would have saved me hours of my life for both my upgrade and my early papers. Identify the reference management software that will work for you early on and then get into the habit of routinely adding any papers you download into the software, so you don't have to do it all at the point where you are trying to write a big document. Using reference management software means that when you are making edits, or moving sentences around, you won't need to manually edit your reference order every time. Manual editing is fine if you have ten references, but you will get to the point where you are probably working with hundreds, and so using software will both save you time and ensure you don't make mistakes which will be picked up by examiners. There are free reference manager programmes, but most universities will also provide access to other options for free which would normally require payment. Have a play with a few if you can, as different ones work for how different people work/think.

The other thing that is worth investing some time in at this point, as this is likely one of your first large documents, is understanding how Word or whatever you are writing in, can be set up to aid you rather than causing you stress. Learning how to use headers and other tools that will enable auto-formation of content pages, figure and table lists, is a great investment of your time. You will need to be able to utilise these skills when you are writing your thesis, and starting to learn them at this point will give you plenty of time to play around and perfect them before starting on one of the largest documents you are likely to ever write, rather than adding that as a learning requirement when you are already likely to be pretty stressed.

All of this brings me onto what might be the most important factor of all, time. In year one you spent a lot of time developing project plans, which should really help with this. One of the biggest pitfalls is that students plan for writing time, but not for revision time. This isn't a document that you should be aiming to send to your supervisor once, you should be planning for multiple review and revision points. Everything from developing your aims and objectives, and framework input, to final finessing. Each of these points will lead to addition of quite a lot of extra time. In general, your supervisor will need at least a week for each one, as they will need to manage inputting into your work in addition to other clashing demands. There are things you can do to help, like providing advance notice of when you are likely to be emailing things over, so they can plan diaries, but there will still be delays. Make sure you include all of this into your timelines in order to give you the time you need to ensure that the document you are submitting is something you are really happy with and gives you the best foundation for the rest of your PhD. Your upgrade/literature review will often act as the basis of your thesis, so take the time needed to get it right.

CHAPTER SEVENTEEN: SUBMITTING YOUR FIRST CONFERENCE ABSTRACT

When you reach the mid-point of your PhD, irrespective of whether you've ended up including pilot data in your upgrade, or whether you've had to upgrade at all, the time has come to start to take your first steps in disseminating your work. This can happen in all kinds of ways and in all kinds of settings, but often it will be by presenting your work to other academics. Hopefully, you will have already had the opportunity to practice this skill a little by presenting to your academic group, and I would always advise that you consider submitting to your local department or university conference whenever the opportunity arises. These are safe spaces for you to develop and then refine your skills.

By the midpoint of your PhD though you are likely to have something that you want to consider presenting on a slightly larger stage. Conference presentations are a good way to start, as although they may require some level of data, they often don't require quite the same level that you would need to start putting together a paper. It is often possible to submit, for example, something based on the literature review that you have already undertaken. Submitting your first abstract for a conference can feel like a massive step, and can also be nerve wracking, there are ways to prepare and help improve your chances of success, however.

The first of these is to carefully consider both the conference in general and the rules related to submission. It can be really helpful to think about a number of conference factors to help you decide whether it is the right conference for you:

- National or international
- Conference size
- Conference cost
- Funders requirements
- Submission timelines
- Submission process
- Poster and/or oral submission options
- Types of poster categories (video, electronic, paper)
- Number of presentation tracks (different sub-topic days for presentations)

- Availability of bursary or attendance support
- Who else is likely to attend

For your first conference submission you are likely to prioritise experience over impact. This is because you will have your best data towards the end of your PhD, and you may, therefore, want to save attending the one international conference you are funded to attend for when you have the best possible data. Both because you want to help get that data out, and conference submission can help your work get picked up by publishers, but also because you are most likely to need to get yourself out there, in order to look for future employment options and career progression.

It is worth prioritising experience therefore for your first presentation. You want to consider submitting to a conference that suits you and your work best. Which conference has the most appropriate presentation tracks? Which conference suits your personality best? If you are an introvert, you may not want to choose a 5000+ person conference as your first. They can be very large and intimidating, and even if you know some other people attending they can be really hard to find amongst the masses. You may wish to choose a conference with a few hundred to 2000 people instead, as they feel much more intimate. You are also best off choosing a conference where you will know other people who are attending, be they your supervisors or other people from your group. Your first conference presentation is a big deal and it's nice to have some cheer leaders who pop by and read your poster or sit in the crowd and start you off with a nice question during your presentation to help make you comfortable.

Once you've chosen your conference it's time to do some research about the logistics of submitting. Lots of people will focus on writing the abstract itself, and that is super important, but if you check out some of the other details first you can really improve your chances of success. This is because, for many larger conferences, submitting an abstract is quite a task in and of itself. To begin with you will usually need to register and create a profile as an initial step. If you want to create a student profile, you will also often need to submit proof of your status, either via a letter from your supervisor or through pictures of your student ID. Some conferences won't let you finalise your registration until these are verified, which will often take several days. Make sure you have started this process early so that you don't find yourself having written a great abstract but unable to actually submit it.

Once you have registered an account, it is sensible to actually begin the submission process, even if you haven't written a word of the abstract yet. Going through this process, even if you just enter nonsense in the boxes, will allow you to make a note of all the information that will be required to have as part of the submission.

Frequently submissions require you to have at least the following information available to complete:

- Author list, in order
- Titles, academic institutions and contact details for all authors
- Presentation option you are applying for (oral, E-poster, poster)
- Dates you will be attending
- Conference track submitting to
- Abstract details (title length, abstract structure)
- Disclosure and right to publish agreements
- Presenting author
- Corresponding author

When you are going through the various submission pages, ensure you make a note of all of the difference conference tracks you can choose from. One of the biggest reasons that abstracts are rejected during conference review is that people choose a conference track (subject sub-category) that isn't best suited to their work. Take some time to really look at the different options and think what your learning objectives i.e. what you want someone to take away from your presentation will be. Then make sure you pick the category that aligns best. This sounds pretty simple, and for novel research that doesn't sit within a multidisciplinary space it often is. However, it can be harder when you are submitting something based on a literature review or when your work could sit within multiple options. Getting this step right reaps benefits, and so it can also be worth looking at programmes from previous years to see what kind of posters they had under the different conference tracks to aid your decision making.

The next thing to take a note of are the requirements listed for abstract title, abstract length, and abstract structure. It is highly frustrating, as someone who has done this, to have written your abstract and title, gotten it all together for submission, and then find that your carefully crafted title is two words too long to meet the criteria. Taking note of all of these requirements before you start to write will remove some of the last-minute hurdles you might face. Although you can submit an abstract that doesn't adhere to the headings requested, this is another common error that may contribute to your submission not being chosen, as it can be seen as a lack of attention to detail.

You are now at a point where you can start drafting your abstract. Your required structure will often give you quite a lot of clues about what it is that is required of you. This can, again, also be helped by looking at the poster abstracts listed from previous years, which are often either published as a special journal article or still available on websites. There are discipline specific variations on how abstracts should be written, for instance in my science/health discipline, abstracts generally don't focus heavily on background and conclusion, with the main amount of the text being split between methods and results. This is because you are presenting in a subject specific category, and so in-depth background is not considered necessary, and you are usually submitting a poster during preliminary work, and so the conclusions are not always fully worked up.

Conference presentations are also quite limited in either time or space, and so you normally have to select only a single strand of your research story, which can also limit wider ranging conclusions. Consciously choosing which specific story thread you want to tell will make writing the abstract itself easier, as well as supporting a more focussed approach to the presentation itself, It is important to note that anything you've submitted as a manuscript or for publication elsewhere is often not acceptable for submission at major conferences, because they want to publish abstracts and the details cannot be subject to existing copywrite. Lots of editors will be present to view work, so presenting is a great way to fast track to publication, but to attract those editors most of the work needs to not have been already published.

To get started, I would always write down each of the headers that have been suggested for inclusion. I would then spend time picking one bullet pointed sentence that I will structure the results section around. Once you have your results 'story', you then write the methods bullet point that states what work needed to happen to reach the result. I would then write my conclusion bullet point based on that single result, what it means and what the impact of it is. You are then in a position to give just enough background in your starting bullet point to cover off the key details needed to be able to understand the rest of what you have written. Only write what is needed to support your story. Once you have your bullet points you can then turn each into short paragraphs, all of which will be focussed as you have already been selective about what it was that you wanted to convey.

I would recommend always drafting your submissions in Word, or some other word processing programme. This enables you to check word count as you are drafting. It will also enable your supervisors and other authors to add comments and track changes. I would always maintain version control, saving under different versions and with different dates, and keeping track using initials or other means, of who has commented on different versions. As part of this drafting, I would also include authors in order, and the title, as well as the abstract itself. Again, author order does change a little between disciplines but for a conference submission there are three main authors of note: first author, presenting author (may or may not be the same as first), and senior author.

This brings me onto authorship. I had no idea when I submitted my first abstract that the order of names on that abstract meant anything. I particularly had no idea how easy it was to upset people if that order of names was not considered to represent the contributions of everyone involved in the right way. The first author will normally be the person who is writing the abstract submission. The presenting author is the person who will be travelling to the conference to present the work, this is often the first or senior author but depending on schedules could be someone else. The senior author is the person who comes last in the list of authors and is usually the person who either conceived the work or who funded the work. Other authors will come between those depending on seniority and/or contribution to the work. I would always suggest you check in with your senior author on how this list should look before sending anything out to comment, as getting it right early can make the entire process easier.

When drafting there are some common pitfalls to avoid. The first, as for most things, is not leaving enough time. There have been occasions where others have submitted my name as an author on an abstract without me having the opportunity to see or comment. This is pretty bad form and usually happens due to time constraints. Allowing plenty of time should mean that this doesn't happen. If you are ever up against the clock, you should always ensure that you have verbal permission from the authors to do this, as by entering their names on the website you are often stating that you have their agreement linked to submission. The other reason you want to make sure your fellow authors have time to see it, is because they should be able to support you in making it better. You want your first conference experience to be great and so make sure you have given your submission the time and attention is deserves to be something you can be proud of.

Finally, when you are there pressing the submit button, try to also ensure that you have also left enough time to apply for any travel or attendance bursaries that you are entitled to. This again is something that gets missed if there isn't much time, but it will enable to you enhance both your conference experience and your CV, as well as getting your name out there, as bursary winners are frequently highlighted.

CHAPTER EIGHTEEN: WRITING YOUR FIRST CONFERENCE PRESENTATION OR POSTER

I often feel like submitting an abstract is the main outcome when I'm working so hard to draft one. The truth of the matter, obviously, is that submitting your abstract and getting it accepted is merely the beginning of the process, with designing, researching, writing and preparation forming the key next steps. The rest of these stages result in a state of anxiety for many, especially when you are at an early stage in your career. The anxiety often comes as we know that conference presentations are important for both getting our work out there, and for personal and career development. Presenting therefore, can feel like quite a high stakes manoeuvre, especially if you are not comfortable with public speaking or being the centre of attention. With this in mind, I thought it might be useful to share some tips for preparing any upcoming session.

Let's start by talking about designing your session. There are few different types of common presentations that occur at conferences:

- Debates
- Research presentations
- Topic presentations
- Workshops
- Plenary or keynote
- Speed presentations (three-minute thesis type sessions)
- Poster presentation
- Career presentations
- Panel sessions

The most common of these for you to be involved with as an early career academic are speed presentations, poster presentations, and research presentations. All of which will have slightly different requirements in how you put them together. For instance, for a speed presentation you will be able to communicate one key thing and that will need to be clearly considered as part of your design process. A poster presentation, however, will need to be able to stand alone without having additional oral information. You will have the chance to stand by your poster and 'present' it to people, but it will also need to make complete sense for those wandering by your poster during the rest of the day when you aren't there to provide supporting information.

The first thing to realise when starting out with the design phase is that we often make presentations about us and what we are trying to say, when actually they aren't really about us at all, they are about the audience, and what we are trying to achieve on their behalf. The first step therefore is to think about the learning objectives for the session. What might benefit the audience most? What are they expecting? What baseline level of information do I need to give them in order to be able for them to understand my key message? Learning objectives act as a guidepost for your design process, which obviously also links into the story aspect you decide upon when submitting your abstract.

One of the ways to help you decide on what your audience might need is to think about the session itself that you've been allocated to. For instance, a poster presentation session is often much less formal than an oral presentation, depending on what type you've been given. Informal sessions are usually much more discursive, so your preparation will need to be broader, as you can't write yourself a script of what you are likely to cover. You'll need to bear this is mind in the design phase, as you may need to think about how you want to include much stronger cues to help guide discussion.

The type of session you are allocated will also dictate a number of other things that you will want to take into consideration during your design phase, as will time slot and room allocation. If you know the venue you are going to you may be able to predict numbers of attendees for instance, if you are allocated a room you may be able to find out whether it's for 15 people versus 1500. High numbers of attendees will limit your options for interactions, as will being given a 15 minute time slot, all of which should be considered whilst thinking about your presentation design and structure. Always confirm with organisers the length of your session and whether this will include time for questions.

For a poster presentation, you should be able to judge how many other posters will be presented in your category at the same time by the session details, which will give you an idea of how many handouts etc you might need to do, as well as if there are competing sessions which will require you to advertise your work via social media. Slots will let you know how stand-alone your poster content will need to be, as they will indicate how much time you will be expected to stand by your poster. There will also be key information for your design provided, such as the poster dimensions, requirements to bring printed or for digital submission, and even whether velcro attachments will be provided to hang your poster or not. As the person who has turned up with a printed landscape poster and had to stand there holding half of it as the poster board provided was portrait, I would advise paying close attention to these details.

Finally, as this will impact your options for engagement with audiences, ask organisers if there will be free Wi-Fi available for attendees so they can access voting apps or poster QR codes? Don't feel like this information should confine your creativity and what you want to undertake but build any limitations into your thinking in order to find solutions ahead of time.

Once you have the answers about your session you can start building upon your initial design thoughts by undertaking some further research. The agenda and available abstracts can help you see what others presenters are covering, especially if they've listed any focuses or learning objectives in their descriptions. This may mean you can get valuable slides back if someone is talking on a similar topic ahead of you, and will therefore have given a lot of similar introductory slides, thus giving you more time to build on the subject in your slot. It can also give you an idea about areas to avoid, so that you don't give too much overlap. One of the things to not do is be intimidated by anyone else on the agenda. If you are speaking/presenting you have earned the right to do so, it doesn't matter if the person before you is Dame X or Professor Y, acknowledge what that might do to the atmosphere in the room (i.e. may mean you have a larger audience) and then plan as if they were any other speaker.

For posters, as well as talks, see if there is a cluster of presentations on a similar theme. If there is, it is worth considering how your work could link into the work being presented by others. It's worth spending a little time researching this, as you may get asked questions, but also because you can then link your poster into the wider context and hopefully encourage more people to come and discuss your work. In general, you should research and start preparing for questions at the same time as preparing your session. I comfort myself by reading up on the areas that I've decided to cover during the design phase, even if it's a topic I know really well, so that I have up to date information and references. I also try to think about the rabbit holes that my audience might want to go down and any potential pitfalls where I might need to practice my response ahead of time. All of these approaches can help ensure you feel as comfortable as possible when you step out to present.

Another way you can help yourself feel more comfortable is to include something that is a little bit authentically you within the presentation itself when you come to write it. This can be levelled dependent on setting, sometimes I just choose a colour scheme or icon that speaks to me. Other things you can include are quotes or images that are meaningful to you. Again, it doesn't have to be something big or in the face of your audience, but something that centres you and makes you feel more like you own the space you are presenting in. Sometimes, however, going big is the way forward. Sometimes, making something memorable is the right approach. It all depends on your confidence level and the setting.

When writing modern conference sessions, and because you are maintaining a focus on your audience, you may want to consider using tools or apps to support interaction with the audience during your session. You can use tools such as Mentimeter and Slido to build voting or other forms of interaction into your session. You may also want to embed things like QR codes into your poster so that it links to papers you've published, or even YouTube content of you discussing your topic.

Even if you are giving a standard presentation without interactive tools you will still need to think about how to engage your audience when writing you session. If you can bring yourself to your session by using framing such as story telling it can really help, alongside the use of humour. You can even think if there are props that would be appropriate to support what you're talking about, although you also don't want to make it gimmicky. Whatever tool you feel comfortable with, practice using it as it will make sure your session is more memorable.

Once you have the nuts and bolts of your presentation done, be that a poster or using some form of presentation software, such as PowerPoint, it is time to get the final stages of your preparation done.

Depending on how you work, and what makes you feel comfortable, you may want to write a script or have notes that you can use to practice with. For posters, it can be useful to have your poster up on a screen and practice talking it through and answering questions from your research group. For presentations, you may want to run through the entire presentation at a group meeting to get a feel for presenting in front of others. Whether you decide to do this or not, you will need to share your version with your supervisors and any contributing authors in order to gain their input. You should think about who you need to acknowledge on your presentation as part of this process, including your funders and university icons. Your university may also have a template that you should be using for any posters or oral presentations, which will help with this and may also save you time in managing design details.

Other facets of the preparation phase will depend on where exactly your conference is, as there are considerations for overseas conferences that may be less important if you are not travelling far or by plane. The first of these is linked very much to poster presentations, and includes considerations like what are your printing your poster on (if you need to actually hang a physical poster), and what will you use to hang it? Printed posters usually require a poster tube to transport them, and you can usually add a poster tube onto the cost when you are printing your poster, so you don't need to source one separately.

If you are flying to your conference, these tubes are often considered part of your hand luggage and depending on your airline you will have to pre-pay for an extra piece of hand luggage or sacrifice a more standard piece that contains your personal items. Booking hand luggage is cheaper if you do it when booking your travel, so think about whether this is necessary early on. One way to avoid hand luggage issues, if you are going long distances, is to pay slightly more during poster printing and get your poster printed on fabric. This means that it will be more robust, and you can fold it easily for travel in your suitcase. Most academic printers can do this on request, but you will need to allow sufficient time for it to be ordered.

This brings me on to something that is worth finding out about early, who is paying for your trip? If you have successfully gained a bursary or travel grant, there may be specific routes through which you need to book and associated timelines. There may also be a need to pay yourself first and then be reimbursed, which can require some financial planning. If no external funding, will your university or funder pay, and what do you need to have set up in order for that to work? For printing, is there a system that you will need to navigate where a specific printer is linked into the university? If so, they may need you to raise a purchase order or have a procurement process to enable this to happen. A similar process may be in place for travel, with universities being linked into a specific travel agent. All of which adds time to any process and will need to be considered as part of your timelines.

Finally, think about how you will handle the unexpected. Things go wrong, despite your best endeavours, so having a plan B in your pocket never hurts. This can be as simple as having a USB with your slides on it. I also always travel with printed A4 versions of my poster/talk to give out. You may never need them, but you will never regret having put the time in to think about and prepare for all eventualities.

CHAPTER NINETEEN: THINGS TO CONSIDER WHEN ATTENDING YOUR FIRST CONFERENCE

Attending your first conference, especially if it's a large one, is both an exciting and intimidating experience. There are so many options about what you could do and be involved with. There are so many people and conference centres can be vast places. There is also a lot that may be completely new to you and require some time to understand how to navigate. It can be easy to become overwhelmed or overstimulated, and that's before you throw in any nerves linked to the fact that you might be presenting for the first time. There's a lot you can do to help ensure your first conference experience in a great one and something that you look back on fondly during future points in your career.

Let's start at the very beginning, arrival. Conferences will often have a fairly soft start, with the first day mostly composed of registration, and maybe a drinks reception. Some conferences even have a pre-conference training offering. It can be tempting to skip these, especially if you have financial limitations linked to your funding and just arrive for the main body of the event. I would avoid this temptation if you can.

There are a number of reasons for this, first, it can mean that you are travelling up on the day you are due to present. I've learnt the hard way that travelling up on the day of a session doesn't work, it just makes me too stressed. There are too many concerns about delays, and then you end up arriving and having to navigate a huge space to find where your poster is due to go up, in very little time. You then discover that you forgot the plastic wallet to attach to the board in which to hold your A4 poster print outs for anyone who wishes to take one, and the organisers have run out of the velcro attachments they were supposed to provide to hang your poster, so now you need to go out and try to find a stationers. All of which feels like a much less significant stress if you have plenty of time to fit in what you need to do. I always advise that you travel up the night before, even if I arrive really late, because then you can go to sleep knowing wants needs to be achieved rather than lying awake all night stressing about whether you will make it to your session.

I would always advise carrying the following with you if you are presenting to address some of the stress, even if you are turning up ahead of time:

- A4 plastic wallet to attach to poster board to hold A4 print outs
- Push pins to attach your plastic wallet etc to the board
- Velco (or other) double sided stickers to attach your poster to the board
- 20 – 50 A4 colour print outs of your poster handouts (you can staple your business card to them)
- 1 A4 print out inviting delegates to take a copy of your poster
- Business cards (in addition to the ones attached to your poster) – if you don't have them from your university, invest in yourself and get your own printed
- Poster tube with your name on it (I have had mine taken when unlabelled)
- USB with your talk and/or poster, to allow last minute printing if there an issue
- Printed copies of your talk, if you are giving an oral presentation
- Notes for your presentation
- Travel iron, if your poster is printed on fabric

The second reason to arrive early is to enable you to get early access to the space and use it to familiarise yourself with the layout. Most large conferences will have an app or a conference brochure which you can use to pre-select what you wish to attend. Sometimes this brochure is only available at the event for collection at registration. Either way you want to ensure you have plenty of time to review in order to make the best possible choices about which sessions work for you. It will also tell you where you will need to be for either your poster or oral presentation.

Once you have been through the information you can then highlight on a map where most of the sessions you are interested in will be running. If you have a couple of sessions you can't choose between, this may help you decide because it is easier to move between closely co-located rooms. Location may also make you re-think some of your choices in very large conference venues, as rooms can be half a mile apart, or even in different buildings, which means that you won't be able to leave one session and arrive in time for the next. Use having early access to the venue to walk around and determine whether the plan you've made is workable, and to identify spaces where you will be presenting in order to become more comfortable with the environment.

Finally, the last reason to arrive early is because that opening reception is worth attending. It is especially worth attending if you won't know that many people at the conference. A common focus of the opening reception is to support delegates networking and meeting one another. This means that there is a focus on circulation and sometimes structures in place to help support people getting to know one another. This can include tables for first time attenders, or topic specific mixing sections. All of which can help you make connections early that can support your wider conference experience. If you miss this session, you will find that other people will have linked up when you are trying to network on subsequent days, and it can feel more intimidating approaching a group than an individual. That's not to say you can't make connections at a later point in the conference, but if you are more introverted it can help to take advantage of these events to make it less intimidating.

This brings me onto networking more widely. Early in your career, conferences can feel very much focussed on knowledge acquisition and development of presentation skills. This is right, you are there to increase your knowledge and awareness of other work being undertaken in your area. One of the biggest reasons to attend conferences though is often missed by this focus on content alone, and that is the networking aspects of conference attendance. The truth is that networking at these kinds of events is essential. Conferences are a fundamental way of hearing the latest science and expanding your knowledge, but they are also key for collaboration and building your networks, as well as dissemination of your work. No matter what anyone says, I have found that academic fields tend not to be meritocracies, there's plenty of 'who you know' involved, and the only way to address that is to get yourself out there. So, you will need to learn how to navigate these settings, and the earlier in your career you manage that, the more rewards you will reap.

A key thing that I have found that supports networking is

something as simple as what I have chosen to wear to the session. One of the things I've come to truly believe is that, no matter how formal the session, you should bring your whole self to it. You should feel free to wear clothes that empower you, and conference sessions are no different. This can be something as simple as wearing your favourite colour, but whatever it is, delivering sessions and attending networking events is easier when you feel good and empowered, so do whatever you need to feel that way. My top tip is that whatever you decide to wear, ensure that it's comfortable. I used to wear heels to speak but now I always wear flats, as I've decided that the pain isn't worth it for me, especially when you consider how long you will be networking after your session. You want to feel comfortable in your own skin and so choose something appropriate that makes you feel good about yourself.

Another way to make networking a little easier is by either booking as a group or joining a society that is having events within the conference. This can help as you are spending time with a much smaller group of people who are likely to have shared interests. You can then utilise these much smaller groups to gradually expand your own networks, as you can then introduce those people to your research group members, and hopefully they will do the same for you. Your supervisors should also play a role in ensuring that you meet others who can provide constructive input into your work, as well as broaden your network to support future career success.

All of this networking and social activity can take its toll, so it is also important to include some downtime when you are scheduling your conference. If you've travelled a long way, you may need to take jet lag into account either on your outbound or return trip. Conference days can be long, some of the American conferences I've been to start at 5:30am and have activities that run till 9pm. You need to strike a balance between engaging with all of the conference material, and ensuring you have enough downtime to support you processing all that you have learnt and experienced. This may mean that you plan to have some evenings off, or you could decide to engage with the social agenda arranged by the conference. Some conferences will run evening trips to venues that align with the academic subject, or even just tours of the city so that attendees can experience some of what the location has to offer. Only you know how to balance your introvert/extrovert tendencies, but make sure you bear them in mind when drawing up your conference plan.

My last tip for planning your conference experience is that you have a think beforehand about how you are going to capture all of the ideas that strike you during your sessions. One of the great things about attending an academic conference is that you will hear and be inspired by so many people. Plan how you are going to capture the thoughts, be that by taking notes on a laptop, or recording your immediate thoughts on a phone post session. You will want to use this time to drive you to create better work, and to reinvigorate you when things feel challenging. Have a way that you can store your responses in an accessible format that will serve you for years, not just for the period of your trip.

CHAPTER TWENTY: GETTING STARTED ON WRITING YOUR FIRST ACADEMIC PAPER

One of the key outputs from any PhD is a published manuscript. If you manage to achieve a paper in a peer reviewed journal during your PhD it makes a big difference to how confident you can feel going into your viva. One of the assessment criteria for a PhD is 'a thesis must demonstrate original research and a substantial contribution to knowledge in the field' and a paper is a demonstration that your work is not only novel, but good enough to stand up to external peer review and add value to the published landscape of your topic area.

Once you have presented your work at a conference, and hopefully received useful feedback, taken questions that have supported your thinking, and maybe even had an editor express interest in your work, the time has come to start working on a manuscript that should tick this key PhD box.

This process can be easier if you have already been involved in paper preparation as something other than first author, but it still feels quite different being the person who is leading and making decisions, in concert with your senior author. I can still clearly remember the stress that writing and submitting my first 1st author scientific paper caused me. I was worried about doing the data justice, I was worried about what would happen if it got rejected, I was worried about disappointing my supervisor. A lot of this was because my supervision was quite hands off, and so I was given space to makes the mistakes and take the learning on my own. It is true that you can learn a lot fairly rapidly with this approach, I would however recommend that you don't go it so alone and ensure that you either link in closely with one of your supervisors, or a post-doctoral researcher in your team, to aid you in navigating the process as it's so much more than just writing.

There are some main stages to paper drafting and submission which are worth bearing in mind:

- Journal and editor selection
- Drafting
- Co-author edits
- Submission

- Revision
- Hopefully publication (if not, back to the beginning)

Many authors jump straight into drafting without really spending enough (or any) time on journal selection. Many PhD students don't do this as they see their supervisors just jumping straight in. That's normally because supervisors know a lot more about the publishing landscape and so already know the background and which journal suits the thing that they are currently working on. The truth is, to maximise your chances of success, you need to choose the right journal for your content. You also have to present your content in a way that will be attractive to the editors of that journal and fits their particular submission requirements. Every journal will have specific topic areas they are interested in. They will also have specific formats they will want you to follow in terms of length, numbers of figures and tables, as well as referencing style. If you start drafting without having an idea of where you are going to submit you will often not put the correct emphasis on your writing to get it into your journal of choice. You will also waste time you could spend on other things, by later needing to restructure what you have already written.

When you are reviewing the journal landscape, start by doing a search for the topic area linked to your research. You should have a lot of these types of papers already from preparing your literature review, and from research linked to your conference presentation. See where your peers are publishing and use it to narrow down your submission options. Once you have found a few that you think might be appropriate, think which one might be the best fit for your data. Go through similar articles, even if based on approach rather than specific topic and look at the length of different sections in order to understand where the emphasis lies. Do they have a long methods section? Do they focus on discussion? How would this fit with the story you are trying to put together for your data? Use all of this information to put together a ranking order of where you will submit to first, and then where you might submit to next if they decide your paper isn't for them.

Whilst you are doing this review you can do some preliminary structural review which will aid you whilst you are drafting. You should make notes of what the titles of the articles you are using as comparison are like. Are they long and very descriptive titles? Does the journal appreciate a witty title to draw readers in? Even basic things, like do they like a title separated by colons? This can then help you in deciding what you might title your final submission. The same should be done by counting how many paragraphs are in each of the main sections, and the section titles they require. You can use this to then know how to split your word count when you start drafting so that you are meeting the in-house style of the journal you are aiming for. If you get the journal review right, you will save yourself a tonne of time later with re-writes and rejections.

Now you have your journal selected it time to start drafting your manuscript. One of the things that can help with this, and making sure you stick to the theme of your paper, is to think about the order in which you will draft your paper:

- Plan your story
- Plan your figures
- Results
- Methods
- Discussion
- Introduction
- Abstract

It can feel counterintuitive to not just write the paper in the order that you would read it, but as a paper is like a lead character in a novel, you have to introduce that character and keep your focus upon them all the way through in order to feel like the story makes sense to the reader. You can't introduce new concepts part way through, so in order to not waste words and clearly communicate your data, it is often best to work from results – discussion – methods – introduction – abstract, so that you can build what you need to include based on your data and the story you are trying to tell with it.

To help with this you need to have a clear concept of what that story is and which aspects you are covering before you start. Writing a paper is a very different experience to writing a dissertation or thesis. The word count is very limited, usually between 1500 and 4000 words, so it requires you to not waste any of those words on something that doesn't support the story you are trying to tell. Unlike a thesis, your paper is a single thread in terms of story (when you are writing a research paper rather than a review paper) and you will want to spend time making sure that the thread you are choosing is the right one. This is especially important if there are a number of papers that will be coming out of your work. You want the papers to build upon one another and tell a larger story when read together, so choosing the order in which they will come out is even more important than when you are writing a one off.

Once you have the concept down, the place to start drafting is your figures. Most papers will have 1 – 3 figures, and these should be able to communicate your story as self-contained items. Your figures are the backbone of your story and are worth getting right. This is a key area where it is important to make sure you a) spend enough time and b) work with your supervisors, to ensure that they are a true representation of the data, but also that they are focussed enough to allow you to clearly express the key outcomes of your work. You are focussing on adding to the current literature as part of your PhD, so know what it is that you are adding in terms of knowledge and value, know the 'why' of your paper.

Once you have your figures, everything becomes easier. Your methods will include how you collected the data to make your figures. Your discussion includes the interpretation of that data and puts it into the context of other research in that area to give your data wider meaning. The introduction introduces only the concepts that are required to understand your results and to link tightly into your topics as covered in the discussion, and your abstract summarised the key points from each area. Working backwards should enable you to bullet point precisely what you need to cover in each section. This will save you time on both drafting and revisions. Investing in the early development pays dividends as you work through the drafting phase.

Finally, in terms of drafting, make sure you are sharing your drafts early and regularly with your senior author. It's OK to send to wider co-authors when it is much more developed, but it is key to success to involve your senior author throughout the process to help guide the development of the manuscript. It is obviously crucial to include your co-authors, but it can be helpful to pick the point at which you circulate to them. If you include everyone at every stage during drafting, you can end up with too many different points of view that mean you end up with a manuscript that is unclear or meandering. Develop the core of the paper with your senior author, and then when the story is sufficiently developed that it will be clear to others, share at that point so the paper is enhanced rather than confused by their input.

The last hurdle to this phase of drafting is submission. Journals will have guidelines available for you to access on the submission process, but it is often only when you are going through the actual online process that what is needed truly become clear. You will usually need to register with an online submission platform, and it is worth doing this ahead of when you think you will be ready to submit. This will let you get used to the platform, as journals tend to require different things, as well as uploads in different formats.

Before you are ready to submit, but when you are a good way through drafting, it is often worth starting your submission process. This means you can look at the different fields and different upload lists that will be required of you, so you can make a list of what you will need ahead of time. Many platforms require you to submit your paper in numerous sections. You may need to submit figures and tables separately. You may need to submit abstracts with and without authors. Some require signed disclosure letters that contain signatures from all authors, others still require a cover letter uploaded. Knowing what files to prepare ahead of time can remove a lot of the frustration that may otherwise feature as part of the submission process.

When you are ready to submit, make sure you allow plenty of time, and do it at the start of a working day, so you have time to reach out to co-authors if you need to get anything further from them. Make sure you know which publishing option you are going for i.e. open access or not. Also, know whether the journal you are submitting to has a relationship with your university so that any publication fees will be covered, usually linked to the university email address you are using to submit from. Otherwise, it can be a shock when your asked to commit to a bill of several thousand pounds if your paper is accepted. Have a folder with all of the different upload documents ready to go, and make sure this is separate from all of your other versions, so you don't accidentally upload the wrong ones.

Once you've gone through and uploaded everything that is asked of you, make sure that you carefully review the PDF that is created, to ensure that all of your figures and formatting have been maintained, and that the versions of everything are correct. Then press that approve button and celebrate. Submitting a paper is a massive deal, and no matter what happens when it hits the editors' desk, it is a moment to mark through celebration. So, close the laptop and do something to treat yourself, but before you do, send the submitted version to all of your co-authors so they can celebrate with you.

CHAPTER TWENTY ONE: RESPONDING TO REVIEWERS

Once you have submitted your manuscript, it will then be reviewed by an editor for that journal. There are then four main outcomes, although two are more common than the others:

- Immediate acceptance based on editors' decision – usually limited to commissioned articles
- Immediate rejection – usually based on journal remits
- Rejection, but with suggested transfer to a sister journal with a better remit fit
- Submission for onward peer review

Now, let's get the rejection option out of the way. Rejection is just part of the process. Papers will become stronger for revisions and contribute more, thus having more impact. Remember that the criticisms may be of the manuscript but are more often linked to how well your submission fits in with the journal remit, hence the need to undertake journal research prior to developing your submission. They are never criticisms of you, or your academic potential. If you receive an immediate rejection, put it in that context and consider this an opportunity to find a journal that would be a better fit. Even better if they have offered a suggestion of a better fit already, use their expert opinion as a head start for your next steps.

I am aware of articles that have been immediately accepted by the editor, but only ones that have been specifically commissioned. The most common outcome, other than immediate rejection, is therefore onward peer review. You will usually receive and update via the submission system that your paper has been accepted for peer review. This process can be lengthy, as it depends on how easy it is for the editor to find suitable people to review your manuscript, and then how long those reviewers in turn take to submit their comments. I have had papers where I've received reviewers' comments in two weeks. I have had others where it has taken 13 months. Commonly, this process will take 6 – 8 weeks, and you will want to bear this in mind as part of any timelines that are set.

Receiving reviewers' comments can be a challenging process, as even if they liked the paper, they will usually be some level of corrections sent. Reading them when they first come can be challenging therefore, as something that you have worked hard on will have been looked over with a fine-toothed comb. Know that most reviewers do this examination with a focus on making both the manuscript and the research better and read any comments in this light. At this point, remind yourself that getting a chance to respond to reviewers is a success in and of itself. I always take a moment to remind myself that this is an opportunity, an opportunity to make something I care about better than it would be without this process, that it's an opportunity for improvement, and that this opportunity is something to be seized and embraced. Who doesn't want to deliver the best thing they possibly can?

No matter how rough it feels in the moment when you first open the email/attachment and read all those comments where the reviewers have blatantly failed to read your carefully crafted wording in the way it was intended, remember this. Being able to respond to reviewers is worthy of celebration. It means you haven't got a full-on no. It means that the reviewers see there is value in what you have done, even if they believe that it could be improved with some tweaking. Anything that isn't a rejection is worthy of allowing yourself a mini celebration, chocolate bar, glass of wine, cup of tea, before you tackle the trauma of starting to make the changes.

My top tip, if you only take one thing from this chapter, is to never respond immediately. Open the email, read it once, maybe twice, to really ascertain what's been said and see the response deadline, then close it and walk away. Nothing good ever comes from responding in the moment. I personally have a 48-hour rule. I will leave that email closed for at least 48 hours before I open it again, during which time I will drink that celebratory cup of tea and try not to dwell. After 48 hours, I'm allowed to re-open and read it again. If at that point I can read it without an overt emotional response, then I'm ready to respond. If not, I will give it another 48 hours. Almost always, after 48 hours, I open it and it's nowhere near as bad as I had originally perceived with my emotional goggles on and I can just get on with a response.

The other consideration is to not wait too long to respond. This can sound counterintuitive considering what I've said above, but waiting too long can make responding harder. This is for a number of reasons. First, there will be a deadline for you to accept or reject what you've been asked to do, and you have already invested a lot of time to get to this point. Two, you want to draft your response when the original submission is still relatively fresh in your mind as it helps with rebuttals and references. Finally, if you need more than two 48 hour breaks to get your head in the right space it's likely that this is feeding into something bigger and you probably need to escalate early to your supervisory team for their input and support in order to help you move forward.

After you have reached the point where you are ready to sit down and start putting together your response you need to decide on how to structure it. This is likely to vary by academic specialism, and there are many different ways you could go about it but below is a standard method which may be a good starting point.

The first thing is to always be polite. Most reviewers are doing it for the good of the academic community. They are, in essence, doing us all a favour. Therefore, when responding to what they have said it's important to recognise that, and to always be polite in your response that you write. You are all professionals after all. Write in a way that you would be happy to read out loud to someone face to face, and structure it a way that you would be happy to receive it. Keep this in mind throughout your response development.

The second is to be sure to read what the reviewers have actually said, not what you think they have said. This is where having a structured process via which to answer the comments to be addressed really helps, as it enables you to read them in a different way, and thus reflect on their meaning.

There are two main pieces that you will work on in parallel, the response to reviewers document and the manuscript in-text changes. The response to reviewers document is where you will take all your reviewers' comments, there will be at least two, break them down, and write a response to each one. This response is where you will list and cross reference to the in-text document any changes made, or evidence your commentary on why you have chosen not to act on a specific comment. The second document is the manuscript itself where you will make in-text changes, then highlight them so they are easily visible to anyone reading your re-submission.

For the response to reviewers' comments document:

- Commence in a word processing programme and have your manuscript title as the header
- Open with a paragraph where you thank your reviewers for their helpful comments (whether you truly feel it or not, this goes back to always being polite, but in all honesty there's usually a lot of good to be thankful for)
- Break your responses down by reviewer:
- A section headed reviewer 1
- Another headed reviewer 2 etc
- Plus, a general one for the editors' comments if there are any
- Within each section for each reviewer, copy and paste the comments received.
- Break down these comments. Some reviewers give you a lovely bullet pointed list, sometimes with line numbers, and so this is easy. Some will give you paragraphs of text where you then have to extract each point and make a bullet pointed list out of it

At this stage, I tend to remove commentary, things where there are no changes requested. This gives you a bullet pointed list to work from. I then colour code this text by reviewer so it stands out from my responses, which I will write under each bullet point. You can also, at this point, identify whether several reviewers have given similar comments, and then you can cluster those changes. I would address them in the order in which they occur. So, reviewer 1 has a similar comment to reviewer 3, I'd respond in the reviewer 1 section and in the reviewer 3 section state, for instance, 'already addressed under reviewer 1 in line XX'. This process enables you to clearly see what needs to be addressed so you can approach it in a systematic way.

The in-text changes within your manuscript are pretty straight forward once you've decided on your approach. This document contains the changes that you make in response to the reviewers' comments in your original paper. For all of these the action is fairly straight forward, you just make the changes within the original document and write a comment in your response to reviewers stating, 'changed in text – line XX and YY'. I tend to highlight changes to the text in yellow and then make sure I cross reference back in my response to reviewers with line numbers, as well as any commentary, so they are easy to find. The main thing to remember here is, once you've completed your response, save off a 'clean' copy without the highlights as well as the highlighted version as many journals will require you to upload both as part of your re-submission process.

Common features that reviewers want added/addressed in addition to academic process include:

- addition of references
- spelling mistakes
- improvements in unclear sentence structure
- other nuance changes

Sometimes the reviewers will want new points addressed, or occasionally fresh data included. At this point you need to decide how much the paper in its current format is important to you to maintain. Normally the additional points made actually really strengthen the paper and it's very worth spend the few extra hours to add in what has been requested, especially as they tend to be points you had in drafts but were forced to lose due to word count. There will be occasions, however, where you disagree with the reviewer on either the fact that certain points should be included or the way they have suggested that they be done. On these occasions you are entitled, to include commentary under the reviewers' comment where you state why you don't feel that it would be a suitable edit. You will need to be polite and clear, and ideally evidence, why you don't agree. The decision will then lie with the editor as to whether they agree or not.

Once you've completed your response, or earlier if you are deciding to rebut points, it's valuable to get a second opinion. I would always advocate preparing your response to reviewers with the senior author of the paper, but once you have completed them you should send your response documents to all the other authors for sign off. This process is important, both to help ensure that you have addressed all the points raised, but also to help ensure that your arguments are robust where needed. Some papers have lots of authors and you, with their support, may not need all of them to comment.

All that's left to do is go to the submission platform and upload your response. The good news is that this phase takes nowhere near as long as getting your initial reviews back, as it's usually just the editor who looks at your responses and decides whether you have addressed what's asked of you. If your response isn't just going back to the editor you will know as part of your initial feedback, as it will state whether your paper is likely to need to go back out for review once the changes have been made. This will take a little longer than going to the editor, but it is still usually faster than the original review period. Once you've uploaded all that is required is to sit back and plan how you will celebrate your first 1st author paper being accepted. This is a watershed moment in any academic career, and you should plan to celebrate it as such. Congratulations in advance and let me know when it happens.

CHAPTER TWENTY TWO: SURVIVING THE SECOND-YEAR SLUMP

Completing any PhD is a roller coaster and crossing the finish line is a huge milestone. There is a lot of road to travel between the start and completion, however. So, I wanted to finish the year two section by talking about one topic that if I had known about when I started might have meant I didn't feel so alone, out of my depth and like a failure compared to my peers, when it happened to me. I'm talking about the second-year slump.

So, what is the second-year slump? The second-year slump is the time during the middle of your PhD when you feel like you've lost your way. It's the time where most students have a massive crisis of confidence both linked to their own skills and whether they can ever complete it. This crisis also extends to the project itself and whether what you are doing will have value. It can be a dark and lonely time where everything feels really hard and very isolating, especially if you end up managing it on your own.

Why does it happen when it happens? The second year is that point in a project when you have been doing it for long enough to understand the scale of the task and are so firmly embedded in it that you see both all of the challenges and all of the faults. You are also still quite far away from seeing the finish line or having outputs that make you feel you are really achieving. Now, obviously the second-year slump doesn't always occur in the second year. When it happens depends somewhat on the time scale of your PhD, so it may be later if you're working part time or undertaking one over a longer time scale. The thing is it has happened to every PhD student I've spoken to at some point and certainly to every PhD student I've ever supervised.

One of the difficult things about entering the middle stage of your PhD is that you are getting to the point where you will be actively comparing yourself against others. Am I doing OK? Am I working hard enough? Am I productive enough? The problem is that every single project is different, and your learning needs as a student will also be different, as everyone starts in a different place. Therefore, comparing how you are doing against others is often a fool's errand. To compound this, you are often benchmarking against peers that are either super enthusiastic as they have just started, or against other peers who are getting outputs (papers/posters) and meeting their success criteria because they are further down the line. Very rarely do you have someone in exactly the same boat to compare against, and yet we are rarely told to not compare against others.

The other thing about the middle of any long-term project is that you are too far away from the end to truly be able to conceptualise what that end looks like, but far enough from the beginning that the true challenges of the task are becoming very real. Rather than being filled with lots of enthusiasm and just an idea that it is going to be challenging, you now know quite how challenging the path ahead will be. At this stage it can often feel like no progress is being made. The increments are so small that you can't fully judge the distance you have travelled, and you are so fully focussed on what is in front of you that you forget quite how far you've come.

By this point in your PhD, your friends and family are often invested in the process, and you will spend a lot of your life being asked 'how's the PhD going?' or 'when are you thinking of submitting?'. Worse, some people may expect you to have a topic of conversation that isn't about your PhD, and when you are going through a period where it is totally time consuming, not having anything else to talk about can make it feel inescapable. People who haven't done a PhD have nothing to really compare it against in terms of giving you the support you need, and so even when people are trying to help it can end up making the situation feel worse. This is often compounded by your supervisor who will have 1001 different priorities and will be trying to strike a balance between pushing enough and (if you are lucky) caring enough about your health and wellbeing to not push too much.

All of which can mean it is tricky during the second-year slump to find anything positive to say. You can't babble on about everyone you've just met or how great it is to start, you often have nothing concrete that people will understand (like papers and posters) to share, and in all honesty this phase of an experimental PhD is often just filled with a lot of failure which can be difficult to discuss for fear of judgement. These things can all make just simply answering the question 'how is the PhD going?' challenging.

Finally, this is the point at which you are developing and learning the most. You're at the point where you are starting to take risks and explore what it's like to do novel work. You are truly beginning to work as an academic, and that can be scary and require adjustment. At the start of your PhD, you will mostly be doing the 'safe' work. Learning techniques and building on work done by others but not initially taking those next big leaps of thought that are required for you to develop your own work. During your second year you are usually going to be making your own intellectual leaps and so the consequence of that is that there is a lot of failure and troubleshooting as you try and work things out. As you grow into undertaking work as an independent researcher, you make that shift into following up on your own thoughts and taking responsibility for planning your work and its development. This responsibility and the fact that your success is intrinsically linked to how well you develop into this new role can be truly terrifying, but it's rarely articulated.

So, if you are feeling low and lonely in the middle of your project, know that it is not you. Remember that a PhD is hard, and that's OK. Far from failure, this is probably a sign you are truly beginning to reach your academic potential. Just be sure to be kind to yourself as you are navigating your way through. Use some tricks to help you to remember how far you've come, and how much you've learnt. If you are starting out, write notes for yourself to read at 6, 12 and 18 months, as a reminder of where you've been and what you had hoped to have achieved, or even just look back at your early notes. Remember this is just part of the journey, it happens to everyone, and you will come out of the other side wiser and stronger for having gone through this process. Hang in there and find your cheerleaders who will help you through.

TOP TIPS FOR SUCCEEDING IN YOUR SECOND YEAR

Your second year is pivotal and can really impact how you come to view your PhD experience. It is also the time when things start to come together and you start to begin to feel like the researcher you will become. Despite the stress of this transition, it should also be an exciting time as so many firsts will be occurring, from conference attendance to manuscript preparation. Here are some things to bear in mind that should help.

Most of the work is in the preparation

One of the biggest things that can help across not just your PhD, but your future research career, is to understand that most of the work is in the preparation. It can be really tempting to jump right in and start 'doing', but in the long run this often leads to tasks taking longer or requiring substantial revisions. Learning and accepting that thinking and reflection is still work, even if it is harder to see immediate progress, will mean that you will move forward more quickly

It's OK to be scared, but do it anyway

One of the biggest inhibitors of progress, especially in your second year when you are trying new things, is procrastination, usually due to fear, or lack of self belief. A key trap to be aware of is thinking that you are in preparation mode when you are actually in avoidance mode. Preparation is key but at some point you do need to move from thinking into doing. This is where knowing yourself enough to be able to both determine timelines, but also what your drivers are, can be really helpful. Doing nothing is a choice, and one that will always lead to failure, so what do you really have to lose?

Learn how to manage yourself and your responses

Learning how to undertake self reflection, and taking some time to understand how you respond to stress, fear of the unknown, and criticism, is an important skill set to prioritise for development early on in your career. There will be periods when your PhD is stressful, that's the nature of the programme, but being able to tell when you are moving from a motivational level of stress, to one that is crippling or requires active management, will aid you being able to schedule in the breaks or motivators you need to keep you on target.

Failure is part of learning, rather than something to be avoided

Too often we have been trained into the need to avoid failure at all costs on our way through academic training. This is probably a very reasonable approach as an undergraduate, or even at master's level. Once you get past that, avoiding failure means you will miss out on key learning and feedback which would have contributed to you improving at the task at hand. You rarely get feedback for things that you are successful at, which means that it can be difficult to determine what made the difference, what you did right. Gaining feedback for papers and grants when they are not successful can actually unlock the door for bigger success down the line, as you then have key information that supports your overall improvement.

Not everything will go well but that doesn't reflect on you

The other learning linked to failure is linked to making it about task, rather than letting yourself believe that it is a reflection on you. It is all too easy to take failure personally and therefore be too emotional to apply the learning offered. Being able to do anything well takes time and practice, so don't make something a value judgement against your competence, when really it is just a step on the journey to success.

Be clear what you need from others when asking for support

A frequent reason why relationships break down, frustrations occur, and delays are caused, is because we don't really communicate what our needs are and assumptions get made. Thinking through what support you need, being clear about how you communicate those needs, and putting in the effort to make it easy for the support you need to be offered, can make a big difference to how easy it is to achieve any task. If you need someone to review your work, be clear about the kind of level of feedback you need, send a diary invite to be clear about deadlines, and be prepared to send helpful reminders, to help ensure your needs are met.

It is always better to be inclusive

It can tempting, when you are starting out, to have a single minded focus on your work and your needs. This is understandable, but where you can, you should try to remember that no research occurs in isolation. There will be plenty of opportunities to acknowledge the involvement and support of others, linked to authorship, or even thank you slides in your talks. Embed gratitude in all you do. Acknowledge the work and help of others. It will cost you little if anything and could make a big difference to those in receipt.

Things happen when they happen

During the mid-phase of your PhD, it can feel like you are busy doing nothing. It can be hard to see progress being made. The thing to remind yourself of, if and when this happens to you, is that slow progress is still progress. Things will happen when they happen, and both you and your project are on your own timeline. Build a relationship with your supervisors where you have developed enough trust to ask 'am I doing OK?' and trust their response. I say to my PhD students that they will be the first to hear if I have any concerns, so if I'm not worried neither should they be.

Celebrate frequently and recognise all of the stages that get you to the big moments

Life is full of big moments, but those big moments are reached by traversing a whole series of much smaller ones. Make time to celebrate the small, as well as the life defining. Not only will you feel better for it, but your work will benefit from the self reflection it supports.

YEAR THREE

CHAPTER TWENTY THREE: UNDERSTANDING YOUR WRITING PROCESS

Welcome to year three! You've done a lot to get here, and this is where you can put a lot of your learning into action, as well as all of those skills you've developed paying dividends in helping both with your thesis preparation and your viva. Year three will contain even more writing than previous years and will require you to tackle probably the largest single document you will ever write in your career, and so it is worth spending some time right at the start to think about and plan how you will tackle such a large writing task.

You've spent plenty of time thinking about how to plan your work, but you may not have spent enough time thinking about how you go about writing, both the process of getting things done, but also how you actually go about it. We all work differently, but the more you understand how you work the more you will reduce your stress around thesis writing. Are you a 'write it up as I go kind of person?' Are you a 'I need to have all the info to decide what my story is before I start kind of girl?'

The first thing to know about yourself is when procrastination is part of your process and when you are truly just wasting time. For instance, I used to get angry at myself for wasting time when I should be writing. I would spend the first three days of any allocated writing slot wandering around and doing anything but putting words to paper. When I eventually sit down at a laptop the words come easily but only precisely because I've spent three days thinking I'm prevaricating. It turns out that during that period of wandering around I was thinking. Thinking about the story I want to tell with my results. Thinking about my top points. Finally, thinking about structure. It is all of this thinking, not all of it active, that enables me to hit the ground running when I come to actually write. I can get up to 5000 words written at a time, but only if I've pre-done all of the thinking first. Turn out that this is my process, but it took me a long time to appreciate it rather than fighting against it.

Now, you are unlikely to write the way that I do, everyone is different. You will have your own process. Some people need to go through a multiple drafting process in order to get to the point where they've clarified their thinking. Other people really benefit from sitting down and talking through what they have in mind, as they feel the benefit from voicing things out loud. Still others find it helpful to make mind maps or graphically record structure. Any approach that works for you is fine, but it is important to know yourself enough to know when you are in 'preparation phase' vs 'procrastination': one is useful to you, and the other isn't.

Not only is it worth thinking about how you will get your word count down in terms of your thinking process, but once you understand how you work you will need to plan your writing schedule around that, so that your schedule works with you rather than against you. If you are someone who needs distraction for thinking time before you start to write, consider what that distraction might look like. Could you still do your thinking whilst organising a lab book, or printing and sorting references? What other tasks could you do that would not interfere with your thinking process? Making a list of these tasks and planning them prior to writing episodes will enable you to avoid dead time, which can impact productivity. It is also worth considering how long you're comfortable writing in a block. Are you able to write for three full days straight? Are you the kind of person who likes to write for a few hours every morning but that would struggle to write for a full day. You would therefore need to plan a more mix and match approach to your task list.

Another thing to consider with your planning is that you will have days when you plan to do high intensity cognitive tasks, and frankly it doesn't work. You will have days when you wake up feeling unwell. You will have days when you struggle mentally, or that the world feels too much. You need to keep an eye on how frequently these days happen, for your overall wellbeing, as an increase in frequency could mean that you need to take wider action. On those occasions when you do have days that you can't undertake what you'd planned it can really help to have a list of tasks that are a bit lighter, brain processing wise. Tasks such as formatting, or downloading references into your reference library, or making your abbreviation list. Tasks that need to be completed and will save you time on another occasion, that will mean you are still moving forward even if the day feels harder than normal.

It is also worth knowing what helps you in your writing process. For instance, I hate to work in silence, I like music or to have some familiar TV running in the background, all of this means that I prefer to work at home from my sofa. In contrast I have students that need to get out of the house and away from all distractions to get the most done, so they tend to hit the library to have a place to work where they can focus. I even have friends who enjoy working in places like coffee shops so they can look up occasionally and watch the world go by, whilst ensuring they have access to caffeine on demand. Writing is not just about knowing your process, but also the best environment for you to work in.

One final thing to consider when thinking about your process is to ensure you identify gateway tasks. These are the kind of tasks that must be undertaken before other dependent tasks can occur. These are everything from the fact that you can't produce a table of contents until you've finished writing, to needing to make your figures for each section before you write the results. Being cognisant of these dependent tasks will mean you won't run into unexpected blocks, and you can avoid added frustration by taking them into account when you are ordering your planning.

Once you understand how your wider process will work you now need to start the process of getting your word count sorted. I don't know about you, but I find blank pages intimidating. I do. I know that I should see them as full of possibility and exciting, but I see them as a physical representation of how far I have to go. One of the first things I recommend, therefore, is get stuff onto that page in the least stressful way possible. You might want to consider during your reading phase writing the key points and linked references down in a Word document. You can then shuffle them by topic. When you then hit your writing slot you will have lots of text to import into your structure, thus avoiding the blank page terror.

The other thing to consider when writing out your bullet points is to think about your writing structure ahead of time. I've spent quite a lot of time writing different types of documents and I've discovered that there are only so many types of underlying structure, even though they often look different. Papers are a great example of this. One main advantage to them is that you can clearly see what that structure is, and you have access to all the information you need to help you. You will also be able to access other people's theses to review, and by choosing examples of what you like you can then match your structure to help with this. Structure will help you write, and you can use bullet points under headers to help develop that structure, i.e. a bullet point per paragraph. If there are three paragraphs in the section you are writing you may use them as follows:

- Paragraph 1 – What's the setting/problem?
- Paragraph 2 – What are the knowns and what are the unknowns?
- Paragraph 3 – What am I going to do? what's the plan of action?

By planning your paragraph structure, you then try to avoid falling down too many rabbit holes and maintain the story you are telling. You can then use the same method when developing the paragraph itself:

- Line 1 – State what you are going to say.
- Line 2 – Say what you have to say with all the associated detail.
- Line 3 – Reinforce your key point and link to the paragraph that will follow.

Doing this means that you're not worrying about what comes next when writing. You're just hanging words off a structure that helps you as well as leading the reader.

Despite knowing how you write, what you plan to write, and how you plan to write it, there will be some days where writing is just not going to happen. This can happen for a bunch of reasons: tiredness, illness, last minute invitations to a cocktail bar. If however, you can't face writing because of writer's block, you may just need to let the frustration with yourself go as it doesn't get you anywhere. Once you've moved past the irritation you may be able to work out the source of the block and find a way through or around. On the other hand, it may be that you need to take some time rather than forcing yourself to push though. If you need to make an active choice to take a break that is OK, but if you've made the choice embrace it, rather than choosing to take the time and still stressing about it. Also, be aware that you only have so many free passes before you are sitting early on a Saturday morning trying to catch up as you have run out of catch-up time during your standard working week. Use your breaks wisely but ensure you are kind to yourself where you can. Your third year is long, and you will need to plan for rest as well as word count.

CHAPTER TWENTY FOUR: PLANNING YOUR THESIS

When you ask what most people think about when you say PhD, almost everyone will talk about the thesis. Surprisingly few will talk about the research and all of the things that have to happen to get you to the point where you actually produce a thesis. You have, however, gone through a lot to get to this point, all of which should hopefully have gained you the skills you need to make writing your thesis just a series of tasks that you can break down into their component parts, all of which you will have had prior experience of. Tasks such as creating figures, writing an abstract, referencing, and undertaking a literature review. If you break it down into familiar parts that you know how to do, it all becomes a lot less scary. Planning and undertaking this component analysis is a key way to make, what can feel like an intimidating task, more approachable and easier to begin.

Depending on what type of PhD programme you are on, the timing of your thesis submission will change. Some programmes will support a full year of academic research in your third year, with the aim to write up, submit and viva by the end of your fourth year. This approach can be funded or unfunded. Other programmes will have you enter what is sometimes referred to as CRS, or completing research status, as soon as you hit the end of your third funded year. This means that you maintain things like library access, and a university email, but you may lose access to other departmental facilities. This can be a specific issue for science PhDs, where you might lose laboratory access.

The reason for this shift is to move you from a space where you are collecting new data and to drive you into completing analysis with what you already have. No one, not you, your supervisors, or the university, want your thesis submission to linger. There's a key reason for this, as the longer your PhD goes on without you submitting your thesis, the less likely you are to ever submit, and so the system is set up to drive you to get it in within a timely manner.

All of this means that at the start of your third year (or equivalent) it is time to sit down and start to really think about how you are going to get from a point of no thesis to thesis submitted – viva done – corrections entered – PhD awarded. If you've followed the advice from earlier chapters in this book you will have a rough road map, but now is the time to sit down and get granular with the details so that you know exactly what needs to happen for you to reach that graduation ceremony.

The first thing to do is establish what is being asked of you. Every university will have submission guidelines, all of which should lay out what is required of you and the timelines you will be required to meet. This will usually include minimum and maximum length of submission, any layout requirements, such as whether you can print double sided, and fonts with minimum sizes. It will also let you know about declarations that you must include, and usually even what colour the cover must be if you are submitting a paper copy.

One key thing to research at this point is whether your university requires a standard research thesis, where each chapter is specifically written to be included, or alternative approaches accepted. Alternatives may include accepting a manuscript format, where you can submit your published papers, usually at least three, and you write an introduction and discussion to book end these and bring them together. In reality, you probably need to have decided that you want to submit utilising papers early, in order to get them published, but it is possible to make this decision later if you have the number of papers you need. Not every university allows amanuscript-based submission, and it isn't suitable for every project or every student, but if it is a route that you can go down you should explore whether it is right for you in plenty of time before your submission deadline.

Alongside technical things about what your thesis must look like, the guidance will also include a list of paperwork that will need to be completed, whether it can be completed by you alone, or requires both you and your supervisors, and gateways that need to be met. This can include whether you have to have so many course credits or completed a set percentage of your student log prior to submission, or whether your thesis committee has to agree that you are ready to submit.

Once you have this information the best thing to do is to create a submission timeline, working backwards from your ideal submission date, listing all of the gateway dates that you will need to hit and what you will need to have decided or completed to meet each of them.

A common example of this may be:

- Complete PhD by Christmas 2026, in order to graduate in January 2027
- University closes for Christmas
- Submit minor corrections by 1st December
- Three months for minor corrections = viva early September (as early as possible dependent on academic year)
- Submit thesis and submission paperwork 6 weeks before viva date i.e. mid July 2026
- Examiner chosen and submitted 2 months before expected submission date = mid-May 2026
- Start of May 2026 ensure all credits/log completed and schedule thesis committee if required
- April/May submit intention to submit document
- Start drafting thesis January 2026 to allow 6 months to write and revise

You can see why early planning is required, as the process to get your thesis written, submitted, viva'd, and accepted, will usually take at least a year. If you have a hard deadline by which you need to have completed the process, either due to funding, or onward career requirements, these need to be taken into account, otherwise it is easy for your final date to drift.

Once you have worked backwards to enable you to see where your key gateway points are, you need to start putting some further detail with each section. For instance, choosing examiners can take some time. Some supervisors support student input during this phase, but others will choose on your behalf and will take care of the choice and submission requirements. Knowing what level of input that will be required of you during this phase will enable you to plan how much time to devote to it.

Something that is a common mistake when undertaking this timeline phase is that you only focus on the things that you need to do. When you are making your timeline, you will of course, have the dates by which you need to have your chapters done, but students often miss the fact that this date needs further detail attached to it. External factors have the capacity to significantly impact your timeline if you don't plan for them. Supervisors can be highly variable in their time to turn around revisions and they can take even longer if they are not pre-warned of timeline requirements.

You will therefore need to have dates where you plan to have your first draft, and then you will need to also include revision and editing dates after this, all to reach your chapter deadlines. It can really help to sit with your supervisor when you are preparing your timeline and ask:

- How many versions is your supervisor happy to see?
- How much time do they require per version for review?
- Do they want to see a complete chapter at a time, or sections/figures as they become available?
- Do they want the submission dates notified in advance, i.e. booked into their diary, so that they can dedicate time within their diary to turn it around?
- How do they want to handle the edits, independently or sitting together and editing in real time with you?

The other thing to do as part of this exercise is to familiarise yourself with what the viva will involve, and if there are any departmental requirements in addition to university ones. Some departments will require you to undertake a presentation as part of your viva day, others will require aspects such as a public defence, where part or all of your viva is undertaken in public. Preparing for these will need to be included in your timeline, often in the dead time between submitting your thesis and awaiting your viva. They mustn't be forgotten though as they will need preparing for as part of your examination process.

One final thing that can help with making your timeline planning as accurate as possible is to undertake a final phase where you cross check and undertake a gap analysis of everything you have already written. At this point, you should have already written a literature review, you will hopefully already have a published paper, and you may have been writing content, like your methods, as you go. All of this work needs to be reviewed so you know how much of it is usable as currently written, and how much of it would be usable if revised, so that you can take account of it in your timelines. This will allow you to devote more time to the sections where you have no pre-existing content available.

Once you have all of this done, you will be in great shape to dive in and start preparing your thesis, hopefully in a way that is fulfilling and brings you joy, rather than a source of intense stress. Writing your thesis can be a great experience, you just have to be ready and able to break it down in a way that allows you to see the way forward. So, stock up that snack cupboard, hit the stationary store, and buy in that caffeine, it's time to get started.

CHAPTER TWENTY FIVE: WRITING AND SUBMITTING YOUR THESIS

You've put a lot of time into the planning and now the only thing that's left to do is write…or is it? The truth is that this phase of your PhD is a lot like the others you've encountered before i.e. everything is made easier if you put in some groundwork ahead of time. If you jump straight into writing you are likely to make the process more challenging and take a lot longer than if you had invested your time wisely at the beginning.

To help with this it is worth considering your thesis work as part of 4 main phases:

- Preparation phase
- Structuring phase
- Writing phase
- Review phase

There may be some overlap between phases, especially between writing and review, but for the most part they are linear, and ensuring that you have completed them in order will serve the best use of your time and prevent unnecessary time consuming revisions.

The first thing that will require some time to think about as you enter your preparation phase is to consider what purpose your thesis will serve. This one may sound a little weird, as surely everyone's thesis serves the same purpose, to convey the work done during the PhD and provide a route for assessment. That is true. However, in terms of longevity, some theses serve a different purpose. For me, as my research area is also in my area of work, my thesis is a manual I still go back to in order to remind myself of how to do experiments, such as decontamination validations. This won't be true for everyone. Some people write a thesis that will never be read again, and so the thesis is written to please their examiners as its primary function. If you want to continue in an academic career your thesis will serve a different function to if you are planning to move into a non-academic career. Ongoing function should be the first thing you consider, as it will dictate several of your ongoing choices.

Once you have thought about the purpose of your thesis, you then need to think about the story that you want it to tell. You may have done twenty small bits of work that you did because they were individually interesting, but when it comes to your thesis it's time to put those together into chapters that read like you'd planned all of them together and tell a tale that hold logical progression from one chapter to another. Your story, like any tale, needs to have an internal logic, where you are speaking to your examiners about how your work developed, with each section building on the last. As you build you can then demonstrate the novelty and contribution of your work to your subject area, finally finishing with your vision of future work.

A basic thesis should run something like a three-part story:

- The foundation, review of the work of others
- Your contribution, how your work has been undertaken in reference to others
- The future, where your work could develop if it were to be continued

As part of your preparation phase there are a couple of key software tools you will want to spend some time in skill development. The first of which is learning how to make a template in your word processing software of choice. There are many reasons why this is useful, but the main one is that by setting up heading types in your template you can use it to auto produce things like content tables, figure lists and table lists. All of which will save you hours of manual formatting if you set it up from the start. It also helps you make your thesis structure look nicer and more appealing to your examiners, as your sections headers and numbering will all be consistent, along with font use and spacing. There are plenty of YouTube and other guides as to how to do this and investing time so this is set up before you start will mean you start from a place of consistency.

The other software tool to get set up before you start writing is your referencing software. There are several different types of referencing software, some are free, and others will often be provided by your university. Different software works for different people, but it is worth bearing in mind that once you start with a specific one you tend to be locked in. My preference is for Endnote, but that's just as it's the one I've been using for over a decade. It may be worth playing around with a couple of options before you start, if you have access to more than one, in order to choose your preference.

Reference management software is useful as it can hold all of the different manuscripts and references you wish to use. You normally need to create a reference library, which is why it is worth doing this from the start, where you download your reference into a particular location. I tend to do this for the paper versions where I have added my notes, so that the references and notes are all in one place. As you download you can also download the citation and can add additional information into the software that can help you navigate. How much information you add is up to you. Once you have downloaded the manuscript and info into the programme you can check that it has all been downloaded correctly, and that the citation appears complete. Once this is done these programmes can then interact with your word processing programme as you write, permitting you to add your reference in the format that is correct for your submission requirements. When you update your reference list, they will automatically adjust the reference ordering as you move through the review phase, rather than requiring manual updates of hundreds of references.

Once you have decided on your rationale and software requirements it's time to start making decisions about thesis structure. There are lots of different ways to structure a thesis, and as long as you obey the broad university rules, the detail of how you do it is up to you. A thesis structure should support the story and purpose of your thesis, and so you should actively choose the best structure to match your thesis rationale. One of the best ways to make informed decisions about your structure is to spend time looking at other people's. This can include asking to look at those written by your friends and peers, ones stored by your supervisor or in your department, and many universities have thesis libraries that are available either in print or online. When you review them, it is best to keep a list of the components you like, as well as the bits you don't. Find inspiration for your way of thinking and actively design the structure of your thesis so that it adds to your message, rather than working against it.

There are plenty of different ways to do this, and you can take any approach that makes sense for your work, but there are a few things to consider:

- Think about having a thesis structure diagram at the end of your introduction to show how your work hangs together, so it doesn't have to be intuited by your examiners

- Think carefully about the number of chapters and chapter in order to ensure they are supporting the overall tale you are telling
- Try to embed being clear about your why and project impact throughout. Be conscious about picking the points where you can make your 'so what' clear
- Rationalise what you should include to serve the story you are telling. You do not need to include every single thing you've done, as this could make it harder to read

You will want to also use this structuring opportunity to map your pre-existing content onto your structure, so that you suffer less from blank page syndrome. You will also want to plan some of the smaller scale structural components, such as what will your figure and table layouts look like, so you make them consistent right from the start, and so when you come to moving them into your thesis it is plug and play.

Now you are finally ready to start writing. We've talked about the technicalities of writing quite a lot prior to this but there are some aspects that are especially worth considering when you are writing a document of this size. The first of which is to decide how you will break down the writing. Are you planning to draft in one large document with page breaks, or to draft individual sections and bring them together later on? If it is the later, you really need to have your templating sorted so that recombination goes smoothly. There are a lot of benefits to drafting in section however, not least because it will make it easier to send completed sections out for review and to combine comments.

This brings me onto the next thing, version control and document backups. By the time you submit your thesis you will likely have hundreds of versions of different components. Versions of different tables and figures, versions of different sections, versions of the entire combined document. All of which will need to be clearly labelled to ensure that you understand which is the latest version, which are the versions for inclusion, which are the versions that contain comments etc. Deciding early on your labelling for version control will save hours of shifting through potential file options to find the one you need. I would generally recommend a mix of version number, date, contributor initials, and descriptor i.e. version V212 combined thesis 23_08_25 with ECG comments. I would also recommend storing and backing up all versions to at least 3 separate places, so that you have multiple redundancy. There is little more heartbreaking than trying to re-create something you've spent hours perfecting every single word choice over.

Unlike other pieces of work, where you will have co-authors, your thesis is solely your own and so it is important to deliberately acknowledge where others contribute to your work clearly throughout your thesis. This can include reference to when others were included in your data collection process or in your data analysis. There is no problem with others being involved in your work as long as it is clearly signposted. You will also have a separate acknowledgment section, where it is considered good form to thank people close to you, such as your family, but also your supervisors for their support. This can look however you choose but try to ensure you don't forget anyone who has played a part in your journey.

During the writing phase it is important that you keep coming back to your plan and ensuring that everything you are doing has purpose and supports the story you intend to tell. It is so tempting to throw in extra bits, but remember, you did all of that preparation and planning for a reason. More is not always better, and if you stray from your core thoughts it is easy to present a confusing finished product to be assessed. Keep to your why, and the whole thing will hold together with purpose and clarity, which is what your examiners will want to see.

Once you have started to complete some first drafts you begin to enter the review phase. This will often work in parallel at some points with your writing phase, as you send pieces out for comment whilst you continue to work on other sections. The key advice here is that you ask for people to return the commented sections with track changes, so it easy for you to see what edits have been undertaken, as well as comments for improvement You will often have multiple people reading and commenting, and unless they have used track changes it is almost impossible to then combine them into a single document. It is also worth being clear whether you will except edits on printed versions with handwritten notes. There are some people who prefer to do it this way, but if you can discourage them, it will make the combination process easier. Otherwise, you end up having to manually re-type sections, which can lead to additional errors. Also, many peoples' handwriting sucks, and can be really hard to decipher, so having it typed can avoid embarrassing conversations.

All of which brings me onto the importance of having critical friends. These are the people you like and trust to tell you the things you may not want to hear but will make your work better. You will obviously have your supervisors who will be going through all of your versions, but it can help to find a couple of these people in addition who will read though and discuss your work with you, preferably ones who will also help edit as they go. You need people doing this who understand what you are doing, and you have pre-existing relationship capital with, so it won't destroy your friendship when they point out that something isn't making sense and you haven't slept for a week. Prebuild these relationships ahead of time during your PhD, nurture them, they will stand you in good stead, not just for your thesis but for life.

When you start to get feedback, be it from friends, peers or supervisors, bear in mind that writing a thesis is a lot like planning a wedding, once you mention it, everyone will just start offering you advice. All of this advice can become very challenging, as the likelihood is that some, if not all of it, will end up being conflicting, especially if you have too much of it. It's one of the reasons that it's an idea to have just a couple of good critical friends, obviously in addition to your supervisors, as otherwise the number of comments can mean it is hard to know where to start. Keep your circle wide enough to be helpful, but not so wide that it makes life harder.

I would also suggest reviewing all of the advice received on the basis of three things before you take it onboard:

- The level of knowledge and experience of the person giving it you in the specific task you are doing – accepting a history PhD's thoughts on your genomic thesis may not be that helpful, although they may inspire a new approach that could work
- Understand the drivers behind the advice – some people will give you advice just because they feel they have to contribute, and some people will genuinely want to help. Not all advice is benign, however, and so understanding the drivers behind it is key
- Evaluate whether the suggestion works for the way your mind

works – some people will have really good suggestions that don't work for the way you process the world or your vision – ideas are like dresses, the same ones don't fit everyone

Be prepared to find your own way forward as you are the person who needs to both write and defend your thesis. Keep enough of an open mind to accept a challenge that will lead to improvement, but don't try to incorporate everything, otherwise you will lose your voice at the centre of it.

Your thesis, like your PhD, is one of the few times in your career where the work should be entirely yours, and at the end of the day you will be the person sat alone in a room to defend your choices. I'm not advocating ignoring your supervisors, they will have huge amounts of experience, and it is always worth getting the benefit of what they have to say. If the crunch time happens, however, you can't use the 'my supervisor told me to' defence when you are sat in that room and looking your examiners in the eye. Your work has to make sense to you and be presented in a way that you can walk someone else through and defend it. There's a reason a viva is called a defence in the US. You will come out of that room all the more developed as an academic because of it, and whatever happens you should be proud of what you've done.

So, be patient with yourself. This process can take months, and sometimes it's hard to see where it will end. There is little like the feeling of joy however when you quite suddenly realise that you do, in fact, have a thesis. Suddenly all the component parts come together, and you can see it for its whole. In the meantime, remember to schedule in breaks to decompress. Your brain is processing vast amounts of information during your writing up period, and it is easy to become obsessive. You need to walk away from a piece of work to see the problems and the gaps within it. Build in coffee breaks and walks in the sunshine. Build in conversations and relaxing time with friends. Try to find joy in writing up rather than it being one continuous slog. You will thank yourself for it later, and your work will be the better for it.

CHAPTER TWENTY SIX: PREPARING FOR YOUR VIVA

Once you've submitted your thesis, you will generally have 6 weeks or so to a) have a bit of a break, but also to help prepare for your viva. Your viva day can become the focus of a lot of stress, but if you use the time to prepare, you won't be going into the day blind and will know what to expect. Your viva is the one time where people will be forced to sit and listen to you wax lyrical on a topic that you know more about than most people on the planet, so far from being scary, if you are well prepared it should be a very gratifying experience. So how best to use this time to prepare?

Let's start with the practical. You are allowed to take your thesis, annotated, into your viva with you, alongside anything else that you think might be useful. You don't want to take huge amounts in with you, as you won't be able to spend lots of time looking things up, but your examiners will reference pages of your thesis so ensuring you have the notes you need can really help. This can be post-it notes with reminders linked to specific statistical tests or techniques; you could also have a relevant paper printout.

In the week before your viva, it is worth going through and making sure your viva copy of your thesis has notes within it that you can use to put yourself at ease during your viva. This is also a good way of re-familiarising yourself with the detail of your thesis, as you may not have looked at it for a few weeks. When you're doing your thesis notes think about highlighting your examiners papers that you have referenced and be very aware of how they have linked into your narrative.

The other practical thing you can do is to make sure you are familiar with the room in which your viva will be undertaken, especially if you are going to need to do a presentation. Do you have access to log onto the computer? Can you get into the room earlier in the day in order to be able to load your presentation? Does it have speakers if any of your slides require sound? Will there be tea, coffee and refreshments in the room? Do you need to make any special arrangements due to access requirements? Where are the nearest toilets located by the room? Having all of this information will help you navigate on the day and be one less thing for you to worry about.

Once you have sorted some of the more practical things it's time to start the other aspects of your preparation. The first of which is to update your literature review. As I've said, there will be a period of weeks between your submission and your viva, so you will want to be up to date with anything that has come out in the intervening period. The second thing is to look up any papers that have hit the press in your academic area or have been published recently in big name journals, even if they are not particularly related to your specific piece of research. Questions related to this aren't usually pass or fail, but your PhD project may be different to where you end up as a post doc and it helps examiners to gauge how you might make the transition to working in academia more generally.

When you are doing your final literature review it is also worth taking a moment to look at the papers your examiners have published more widely. They will likely have published papers adjacent to your work which you may not have referenced. Be aware of these and where the conversation topics may therefore drift to in order to help you be prepared for the kinds of questions they may ask of you. If you have time, you may also wish to check out who they referenced. We all have go to references and authors, your examiners are no different. By looking at the reference lists in their papers you can see who their go to authors are, and you can see where any overlaps with your work exist. Also, be prepared for questions if you haven't cited the same papers.

Then it's onto the thing that is likely to help you most out of any prep, undertaking at least one practice viva. Whatever your situation, it is always worth having a practice viva, preferably with people that scare you just a little. Ask that amazing post doc who has always been a little intimidating or the person that always asks good but challenging questions at lab meetings. You don't want to destroy your shaky confidence at this point but if set yourself a challenge you will be amazed at how much easier it is when you are in the room for the real thing.

Ideally, if you only have one practice you want to have it with your supervisory panel mostly because your supervisors will know the strengths and weaknesses of your project intimately. They will therefore be able to ask all the questions that you hope your real examiners will skip over or not pick up on. The purpose of asking these questions is not to discredit what you've worked so hard on, all work has weaknesses, it's to help you develop a strategy to answer those questions.

A common question is 'if money or resources were no object how you would change the work you have done so far and how would you plan the next steps for your project?' You will have had plenty of time to reflect on the weaknesses of your work, this is the moment where you get to talk about how you would address those weaknesses by discussing what the next steps for your work could be. Practice both a realistic answer 'I would put in a grant to X funding body to continue Y aspect of my work because….' as well as developing a super ambitious version for if someone took away all of the resource limitations placed upon you.

Now, as part of your viva prep you will probably learn to answer some of the difficult questions like a politician, where you acknowledge the questions and then deflect to a strength when following up. This is different to just not answering the question. Hearing and understanding the question being asked of you is a skill, and worth being consciously aware of. Hearing the question can be especially tricky in a PhD viva when the questions may be long and multi-component. Consider taking in a pad of paper and pen so that you can write down sections from multi-component questions (just words as prompts) so you can ensure that you answer everything asked of you. Also, feel free to ask for questions to be repeated so that you are sure you have clarity before you start to speak.

It is also worth remembering that in a PhD viva you are also able to take the lead in some of the discussion. This is your chance to really talk about your work after all, but it's important that you bear in mind the point you are trying to make rather than meandering or going down rabbit holes. If you go off topic too much it can give your examiner doubts about your ability to prioritise key points, which can indicate a lack of thorough understanding.

If you don't know the answer please just say so, it's OK. There is nothing worse than having someone try to pretend they know the answer or watching them actively make things up in a viva. Academia is about the unknown and there will be numerous points in your working life where you don't know the answer. If you try to blag, it can indicate that you might not acknowledge key failings or points in your work/field that you don't know/understand, not just in your viva but in your practice. This can be a red flag and will mean your examiners push harder and dig more to uncover what other weaknesses may be present. It is perfectly fine to acknowledge that you are having a blank and would prefer to come back to a question later or say that is not something you have a concrete answer for, but you would consider X, Y, Z in finding an answer. Practice responding to questions you don't have the answer to, it will stand you in good stead for your viva, but also for conference questions and other situations in the future.

Another area where it might be required for you to practice your responses is linked to acknowledging the role of others in your work. A lot of PhDs contain sections where you supported rather than led on research, especially as part of early pieces of work. You may have had some statistics, bioinformatics, or sampling support. It is OK to have work that has been co-created or even led by others, as long as this is well acknowledged and there is enough in your thesis that is unique or led by you. Hiding these contributions or playing them down may make your examiners question the level of your contribution and cause them to want to explore this area further. Being able to work with others is a strength and not a weakness, so practice being able to clearly describe your role, your contribution, and your learning, as part of your viva.

Finally, it is worthwhile spending some time practicing how to talk about yourself, your learning and your future ambitions. Although PhD viva exams can feel like they are all about the data that's not actually true. They are also about you as a person, not just the research. It is important therefore to be prepared to answer questions to help the examiners get to know more about you. What was it that made you want to do a PhD? What were your skills and interests when you started? What were the learning outcomes that you were aiming to complete by the time you finished?

A PhD is effectively an apprenticeship in research with the aim that you will become an independent researcher at the end. All that is about more than just data collection. What skills and techniques do you feel like you've picked up along the way? What other transferable skills have you learnt? Have you mentored master's students? Presented at conferences? Written papers? Have you undertaken any science communication or public engagement – what have you learnt? Which courses have you undertaken as part of your PhD? What networks have you become part of? What collaborations have you formed? Thinking and preparing to answer questions like this will give your examiners a much greater idea of where you came from and help to benchmark how far you've come.

You should also be prepared to talk about your plans for the future. Are you going to stay in academia? Are you interested in transferring to industry? Would you like to become a clinical academic? This a great way to help examiners understand why you may have made some of the choices of direction you've made linked to project, for instance taking a more clinical bent. It is also a good way to have a conversation that may help your thinking about where you want to be in 5 years and if you're lucky gain advice from some very experienced people on next the steps.

Practice makes perfect, and the more practice you can have the better. Don't let the practice be a source of stress however, let it be a way to hear how different people phrase the same questions, and to learn how different people pick up and focus on different things. Your viva should be a conversation, and you should feel empowered to bring yourself fully to that conversation. You have written thousands of words on this topic, your viva is merely a chance to let what you know shine, so feel confident walking into the room because of all of the work you have put in to get you there.

CHAPTER TWENTY SEVEN: EMBRACING YOUR VIVA DAY

Your viva day is finally here. I always tell my students that it is a day, that despite feeling understandably stressful, should also be a day to be enjoyed. No matter how many times your supervisors and others tell you that it will be OK, you won't believe them, but you've done a lot to get this opportunity, and I hope that once it is done you will be able to look back on it as a fond and watershed moment for your career. The run up to the actual event is therefore, mostly about keeping yourself calm, centred, and positioning yourself to do the best that you can once you step into the room.

How the actual day of your viva goes can in some ways depend upon the timing of the viva itself. If it is the morning, you won't have very long to build yourself into a worry, but it is harder to predict the length of time of the viva. If the viva is in the afternoon, it is more reasonable to predict the viva will be over by the end of the working day, and therefore to guess at how long you will be in the room. Your supervisors may have extra information, as they may have been involved in booking train tickets, or conversations about a post viva lunch or dinner, which may also help you judge. In reality, this is all just speculation as you can't control what happens once you step into the room, but it can help give you a framework for managing your expectations. Most universities will have a minimum time for a PhD viva, usually of at least an hour, and most viva voca I've been involved with last around 3 hours, although up to 6 hours is not uncommon.

Don't worry about breaks and refreshments though, your supervisors should normally have arranged refreshments and snacks to be present in the room, both for yourself and your examiners. You should always feel empowered to ask for a break, either to have a drink or to head to the bathroom. If you have particular requirements, due to an underlying condition, your supervisor can also arrange for you to have regular breaks during the viva itself. Everyone wants you to be at your best, and so it's about supporting you to be present in the room.

It is easy to spiral in the run up to the viva itself, and so it may be useful to remind yourself of a few things. First, most universities require your examiners to present a report at least one week before the viva itself. In this report your examiners are usually required to recommend whether the thesis itself is of a level that would justify the awarding of a PhD. This means that you shouldn't reach the point of walking into the viva room if it has already been determined that your thesis is not of sufficient quality to meet the standards. I would expect that your supervisors would therefore have taken you to one side, alongside other university staff, to talk about what the next steps would like, without putting you through the viva.

The other thing to consider is that you will have gone through a number of gateways in the lead up to submission of your thesis to determine that you were on the right pathway to enable to success. This will include approval from thesis committees, external verification of your project via upgrade or other steps, and the expert opinion of your supervisors. Most supervisory teams will have seen multiple thesis between them but will also have gone through the process with many PhD students. They will not wish to put you, as their student, through a process that they don't believe you are ready for. Your success is also their success, and it looks badly on supervisors when their students fail. They will only have put you through submission therefore if they believe that you are ready and so have faith in their knowledge and expertise to judge that you are well placed to succeed.

Know that it is also OK to be nervous, everyone expects it. A lot of people go into the examination room thinking that it will be adversarial setting, the opposite should be true, we are rooting for you. Our job, as examiners, is to support you through the process to get the most out of both you and your work. Everyone understands that you will be nervous, everyone in that room has sat on the other side of the table, has sat in your shoes, they know therefore both how it feels and what it means. Believe it or not, but your examiners are often also a little bit nervous. Everyone is aware of their responsibilities and wants to do the best job they can. So just be prepared to take a deep breath and focus on your work, as well as how far you've come since you first stepped foot into the department.

One of the things that can really work to enhance your confidence and comfort, is to think about what you plan to wear on the day. This may seem like a given but it's really useful to think about how you want to be perceived in the room. How much this matters, in part, is dependent upon some of the research you've done. There are some examiners who would immediately think less of you if you turn up in the room and aren't suited and booted, so it is worth checking in with your supervisors about expectations. The main thing, in terms of clothing and outfit, is that it's important to be comfortable, whatever route you choose to go down. You may be sitting in that outfit for 6 hours and so you don't want to have to constantly be adjusting necklines or moving waist bands that are cutting into you. You need to be in the moment and so choose an outfit that helps that by making you feel comfortable in your own skin, preferably professional enough that you don't risk upsetting anyone. You may find wearing a T-shirt under that top that sums up who you are is helpful or having a mascot in your pocket that you can slip a hand into and grip if it gets stressful is helpful. I genuinely don't believe there are any hard and fast rules here other than to plan it before hand and make sure you give your outfit a dress rehearsal to make sure it empowers rather than distracts you.

To be honest appearance isn't something that is important to me when I examine, being present and polite in the room is way more important to me. I find body language is really key in this kind of face-to-face assessment. You really need to be aware of what your body language is saying. No matter how you feel it's going it's important to stay open, smiling and responsive in terms of your body language. If you have a 'resting bitch face' it's worth being aware of it as you don't want to come over as angry or defensive when you are dealing with the questions. Mostly because you won't get your point across anywhere near as clearly as it will be distracting for the examiners.

If you feel like you start to lose control or react in a way that isn't ideal then ask to take a break to compose yourself, or even just make sure you start to take sips of water before you speak in order to centre yourself. To be honest, taking a sip of water before you speak is a good plan in general. Responding too quickly can mean you either don't think through your response or forget some of the lessons you've learnt in your practice viva. Be prepared to calmly justify your decision making and don't throw yourself under the bus by panic responding in a way that points to holes in your work unnecessarily.

Don't be afraid to talk about challenges you have faced, in fact you will often be asked to talk about the biggest challenges within your project. It is important to think about what you want to discuss in response to this question: what was the challenge? how did you respond to it? what was the learning you took from it, both about yourself and the work? These questions are important for the examiner not just to understand what your progress to viva has involved but also how you think and respond. This is a great opportunity to talk about things that matter to you and to help the examiners get to know who you are as a researcher. Stay open, stay engaged and stay hopeful.

Finally, this is a big one. No matter what happens in that room know that it is rarely the end. For good or bad almost everyone comes out of that room with further work, with something more to do. That is very much part of the learning. A lot of people who haven't done a PhD think that the viva is the end of the process, the big hooray, but I must admit it didn't feel real to me until I stood at a graduation ceremony in my graduation robes knowing it was truly done.

Whatever happens you will walk out of that room with a whole bunch of concrete information that will allow you to put a bow on what will already be (probably) one of the best pieces of writing you will ever do. You will also have learnt more than you could dream in the process of prepping for the viva and during the event itself. You will come out of it as a stronger, better person who will have learnt so much about yourself and what you can really achieve when you put your mind to it.

So as much as any oral exam is terrifying, know that you will actually benefit so much from the process. It's one of the few moments in your life where people will be forced to listen to you talk about a topic you will know more about than just about anyone in the world. Enjoy the captive audience and if you can try to be in the moment and make the most of the experience. Then when it's all over make sure you plan to celebrate with your cheerleaders, the ones who've kept you going when the days have been hard, and when it's been challenging to find the way forward. Celebrate, not just for yourself and your learning, but also to give back to those who believed in you, even when you couldn't. No matter how you feel when you leave the room, your supporters deserve to have this moment with you to mark how far you've come, and you deserve to mark the moment.

CHAPTER TWENTY EIGHT: MANAGING YOUR CORRECTIONS

You've made it through your viva. You will normally be told the result on the day, immediately at the end of your session, with further details to follow that list the details of any specific corrections or actions required. Your examiners will usually give you the headlines, along with your supervisor, in the room but no one really expects you to remember them, as most people are just flooded with relief that the exam is over. Your internal and external will then converse independently from you and your supervisor to draw up a list of changes that they wish to see made to your thesis.

So, what happens next? Well, that does in large part depend upon the viva outcome. The outcome dictates what your timeline is for your corrections, as well as who needs to see them to sign them off, and any further stages required. For most outcomes, your internal examiner (the one from your university) will sign off that they are content with the changes made and recommend you for award of your PhD.

The categories and terminology for outcomes change slightly from place to place, as do the timescales for corrections, but broadly include:

Pass without corrections - This is an unusual outcome, but I am aware of a few cases where this has been achieved. It is where your thesis satisfies the requirements for the award of a PhD as is, and no further corrections are required.

Pass with editorial corrections - Not everywhere will have this as a category, but it is where your thesis contains minor editorial and presentational errors, spelling mistakes, missing headings or other changes to be made for the sake of clarity. Usually changes need to be made and resubmitted in quite a short time frame, around a month.

Pass with minor corrections - Minor corrections can be a bit of a misnomer here, as minor corrections have the potential to include quite a lot of re-writing work. The main thing about minor corrections is that they shouldn't require you to do any additional research. You may need to do some minor statistical adjustment, but most of the work you are being asked to do is linked to writing additional text, reworking figures that already exist, or adding in additional references. Depending on the university you will normally have somewhere between 3 and 6 months for these to be submitted. Often, if the changes are more substantial, such as re-writing an entire chapter, you are given the option of choosing between minor and major corrections to give yourself additional time.

Pass with major corrections - This is usually given where additional research is required in order to meet the standards for the awarding of a PhD. As this requires access to university resources to undertake the extra work, and it is acknowledged you may need to do this alongside other demands, you are usually given an extended period of time in order to meet these requirements, often around eighteen months. This can also be what you choose if you have substantial minor corrections and are already in a position where you may not be able to work on them full time, such as already having a job lined up. A pass with major corrections may still only need to be signed off by an internal examiner.

Referral or re-submission (with or without viva) - This is where the level of corrections needed will require that your work is reviewed again, both by an external and internal examiner. In this case your examiners recognise that your work hits the potential standard to meet the award criteria but does not yet meet them at this stage. You will normally need to re-work your thesis, likely with additional research, and then go through the submission process again. You will be told when you have this outcome whether it is a case of just re-submitting your thesis, or whether you would need to go through the viva process again.

MPhil award on PhD submission - This outcome is less likely for universities where students go through an upgrade process, as candidates will have already been examined and viva'd to determine that their projects are suitable for a PhD rather than an MPhil. It is possible that a project may not be suitably novel for a PhD but still has merit enough to be assessed for its research outcomes. This is one of the circumstances where I would expect supervisors to speak to their student before the viva went ahead in order to discuss possible options and ways forward.

Fail - There are very few circumstances where I have known the outcome of the thesis submission to be an out and out fail with no opportunity to revise and resubmit any work. This has usually been due to uncovering of factors that mean the candidate is ineligible, i.e. having paid other people to either do their work or write their thesis. Needless to say, this outcome is very uncommon and shouldn't really be a concern for students that have put in the work and gone through the process.

The most common outcome for any viva is minor corrections, although a fair number of students end up choosing to take major corrections instead, just to ensure they have time to complete the work. The main thing is that for the majority of these outcomes you have a definitive list provided to you to work through, and as long as you demonstrate that you have done the work, it is usually a straightforward process for your internal examiner to sign off when submitted.

The process of doing your corrections is remarkably similar to responding to reviewers' comments, and so if you follow a similar process, you will meet most examiner's needs. Your supervisor will be invaluable in helping you navigate these, but my main recommendation is to allow yourself to celebrate the moment before you start to worry about them. Let yourself enjoy your accomplishments before moving onto the detail of any improvements. My only other advice is not to get so in your head about them that you wait too long. Allow a week or so and then get on and tackle them logically. Do it when the conversation is fresh in your mind and you remember what your examiners meant. Do it calmly and with determination so you can move onto the next phase of your career. Do it before life gets in the way. This is the last hump to get over, so keep your eyes on the prize and focus.

CHAPTER TWENTY NINE: MAXIMISING YOUR OUTPUTS

After multiple years, a thesis, a viva, and then corrections, you may think that your work is done when you finally upload your accepted thesis and wait for your certificate to arrive. Sadly, this is far from true, especially if you want an academic career. Your thesis is a wonderful output, and by far the most important for you as an individual. For your field of work though, and for your ongoing academic career, you need to take the time to make sure that you maximise the other outputs from your thesis, most likely in the form of breaking down chapters of your thesis and reformatting them into further papers for journal submission.

This can feel like a draining task, especially when you have just been through so much, and a period of such high intensity work, but it is something that you will thank yourself for in the future. I say this as someone who didn't manage to invest the time post PhD she would have liked, as I jumped straight back into clinical work. Having taken the time to create the figures and put so much work into reading references and pulling together great text, you owe to yourself that the work done has longevity beyond a thesis that only a handful of people will read.

It will never be as quick, or as easy to get papers out, as just after your thesis submission. Your work will be fully referenced and so adding in a few new papers here and there should take minimal time. Figures, the part of any paper that require the most time to get just right, will already be done. That just leaves you to take the text you have written as part of your thesis and transform it into text for a paper. This is the bit that can take a little time, as you will need to split your very in-depth text from your thesis into single strands of thought that might be appropriate for a paper. That said, as you are so familiar with your text right now, it will be much easier than if you try to do it later with a gap that means you have to remind yourself of your work.

There are also practical reasons to make sure that you try to get on maximising your outputs as part of your completion process. The first of which is financial. Publishing papers costs money, often thousands of pounds. Many universities will have publishing arrangements where they cover the costs, but how this is implemented is usually linked to your university email address. Therefore, if you submit a paper and it is linked to a university email, you don't get charged. Your university email will only work for a defined period post the submission of your thesis however, and you will therefore need to aim to submit everything needed whilst you still have access.

The second is that you will require co-author and supervisor support. I am still in touch with many of my previous PhD students, but there are ones that I don't really hear from. Depending on your relationship with your supervisor, and what you have planned for next steps, you may put variable amounts of effort into maintaining that relationship. Now, I would always recommend that you do what you can, you never know when you will need a reference or when a collaboration will be mutually beneficial. Whilst your relationship is still strong, and whilst you are both invested in the work, is the best time to get outputs sorted. Academics face enormous workloads and challenges related to spinning multiple plates, if you demonstrate that you are keen to continue to make the most of your work and to add value, they are more likely to invest the time needed to make your outputs happen.

The third reason is linked to you now showing that you have the ability to be an independent researcher. The first aspect of this is demonstrating that you are self-motivated enough to maintain an academic career. This is obviously important if you want to stay in academia and is a really important factor when you are going to job interviews, applying for post-doctoral positions. It is also important if you are applying for research funding and potentially post-doctoral fellowships. It can be important even if you are not applying for academic roles, however. If you are applying for the type of roles that require a PhD then they usually have a list of expectations matched to that requirement. These include project management and communication skills, but also that ability to deliver and disseminate, which can be demonstrated by publications.

Outside of papers, there are other things that submitting manuscripts allows you to do, that can help with your wider learning and impact. The first of these is that publishing generally is how you get added to lists of potential reviewers for different journals. Acting as a reviewer is important for a few different reasons. One of the main ones is that reviewing papers is a great way to develop your critical evaluation skills, and therefore to learn how to write your own papers better. It is a great learning opportunity, not just for keeping up with the subject matter, but on learning what to do and what not to do when writing papers, grants etc. After you've submitted your review, you will also have access to the reviews of others, and I still find this a great learning and benchmarking opportunity to see what others have taken from the same paper. By doing enough reviews you'll get to the point where you already hear reviewers' comments in your head as you are writing, thus, your papers will become better as a result.

I always try to review and write comments in a way that is clear and actionable for authors receiving the comments. Try to write in a way that you would like to receive them if the submission was yours. You should also think what is important to consider for inclusion and exclusion in your review. Most journals, for instance, want to know whether the level of writing is good enough for publication, but I would never cross the line into making comments about the English skills of the authors. It's crucial to consider what it constructive and what is not as part of this process. When writing a review, it is important to think 'is it helpful?' 'is it kind?' You are also, however, acting as a gatekeeper, so you should not let papers through for the sake of it.

Finally, think about if there are there any other outputs you'd like to achieve, linked to your research, but also maybe not. I decided to start the Girlymicrobiologist blog shortly after finishing my PhD, and it has taken me to places I couldn't have imagined, including writing this book. You have completed a huge milestone and just like at any milestone moment it is a good time to reflect on what you have learnt, and what you want moving forward. You have done the thing that at times you probably thought you could not do and now you have the opportunity to embrace a new challenge. So, continue to aim high, believe in yourself and do the things that scare you.

TOP TIPS FOR SUCCEEDING IN YOUR THIRD YEAR

During your final year your thesis and your PhD will become all consuming, not just because there is quite a lot of work to get done, but because it can be difficult to switch off your mind and stop thinking about the scale of the project you are currently tackling. There is part of this which is inevitable and probably required to get your thesis over the finishing line, but some of it can be avoided by building in breaks, distraction, and being aware of the detail of what is coming your way so you can plan appropriately.

Your thesis is your thesis

One key thing to remember is that your thesis is your thesis. This means that you hold the responsibility for planning it and getting it done, but it also means that you have a right to do it in a way that works for you. You are the person who will need to sit in a room and defend it, which means that you are the one who needs to be able to talk through how decisions were made. You can, and should, take on the advice that you are given, but this is one of the only times that you are writing something that is very much yours. Don't be afraid to own that independence.

Be prepared to justify your thinking

The counter point to owning your thesis is that you need to be able to talk through everything within it. This means, not just the way it's written and how the work is structured, but also everything that led up to it. Within my scientific world, that includes why you decided to carry out your experiments in specific ways, but more widely expect to be able to justify all of your decisions and explain your thinking. This means that responding that you 'followed supervisor advice' will never be sufficient, so if unclear make sure you clarify ahead of any write up period.

Keep one eye on the future

Having spoken so much about the need to focus, I think it's also important to talk about the growth and development that you will be going through that isn't to do with your thesis and viva. During your third year you will need to keep one eye on the future. Although it can be difficult to find the time, it is key to maintain your connections during this phase, not least of all because you will need to be making plans for what your post viva career will look like. If you are thinking of post doctoral positions, it will be grants that are submitted whilst you are writing up that you will need to be positioning yourself for. Being open about timelines and ensuring that you keep an ear to the ground so you can be aware of what submissions are going in, or to ask about who might support a fellowship application, with be critical to your onward career decision making.

Knowledge is power

Keeping linked in and informed doesn't just apply to future job opportunities. Owning the submission process or your thesis, and therefore being in the driving seat, enables you to feel in control of the process, which can be important psychologically as you progress through. It avoids surprises and allows you to be clear about what you are asking for, and to include any required support within your timings. Knowing that the onus is on you to find out the required information is a healthy practice to develop, as the same will be true for grant submissions and promotion applications, throughout your academic career.

Spend time thinking about what brings you joy

When you are keeping one eye on the future, it is worth being aware during your day to day of what brings you joy. Are you a people person who loves interaction and mentorship? Do you love hitting the library and just spending hours digging through papers and references? Does presenting give you a real buzz? Awareness of what brings you joy will allow you to prioritise some of those aspects when making your onward career choices. There will always be some parts of your job that you won't love, but if you can find roles that allow you maximise what you do, then you will be giving future you a gift.

Develop systems that help rather than hinder

Whether you stay in academia or not, you are likely to face big projects again in your career. One of the reasons people with PhDs are sought after by recruiters is because they have the transferable skills to enable them to succeed outside of the academic environment. Developing systems that you will be able to bring with you into your future career environment can really aid future success. Try to ensure that you build systems that span different projects, rather than only serving an individual need, as it will save you energy both during your PhD and in the future.

Don't get overwhelmed by the big picture

One reason your final year can feel hard is because every task feels so large, so momentous. Writing a thesis is a big task. Sitting a viva is momentous. As these moments are not only big, but feel filled with possible judgement, it can be easy to feel overwhelmed. Know that some days it's OK to ignore the big picture and just focus on a single thing that is directly in front of you. Whether that is one simple task or doing something for yourself to help relieve you of some stress. It doesn't have to be all big all the time.

Keep things in perspective

Something that helps with being overwhelmed is to remind yourself of what really are the consequences if the worst happens. Most of the time, the consequences are linked to inconvenience or possibly some level of embarrassment at most. No one is likely to lose their lives as a result of you gaining major rather than minor corrections. If a paper is rejected, it doesn't mean that it is rejected for ever, it just means it needs some work before you send it elsewhere. No matter what it feels like in the moment, the world will continue to spin and so remind yourself that you will be OK irrespective of the outcome.

Maintain momentum at all costs

Whatever happens, no matter how it feels, just make sure you continue to move forward. Momentum is the one thing you don't want to lose, so just keep putting one foot in front of the other, no matter what. Everything else will just come together.

SECTION THREE – USING YOUR PHD TO SPRINGBOARD INTO A BRIGHTER FUTURE

CHAPTER THIRTY: NAVIGATING THE ACADEMIC LANDSCAPE

During your PhD your thesis can become all consuming. It is, understandably, the focus of your life for years. It can be easy, therefore, to have everything in your working life revolve about your research and have everything feed into getting it submitted. As I've said, it's understandable. The truth of an academic career, however, is that it is about so much more than your thesis and research. There are so many other key skills, or actions that need to be embedded for you to come out of your PhD in the best position to thrive in the academic job market. Section three of this book focusses on these aspects, and how you can maximise your experiences of them during the doctoral phase of your career. Laying good foundations now will pay off in the long term, so trying to make sure you are not so focussed that you ignore them is an effort worth making.

To position yourself for success it is important to understand the landscape you will be working within after your PhD. There are a number of ways to navigate through this landscape, and the decisions you make will impact what your ongoing pathway looks like. After your PhD, many people will choose to think about attaining post-doctoral experience, commonly called post doc posts. These posts tend to last for between 1 and 3 years, and you would normally aim to get at least two of these under your belt before trying to apply for the next steps on the academic ladder. Research isn't the only onward pathway within the academic landscape, however. You can choose to go down a teaching route, where most of your hours will be linked to providing support for, and eventually leading on academic course provision. Or you can choose to undertake the more pastoral and administration aspects of a university progression. Needless to say, you could also choose to leave academia all together, but for this chapter we are going to focus on the academic landscape.

The typical progression if you stay within the research arena is:

- PhD Student
- Postdoctoral Researcher
- Lecturer
- Senior Lecturer/Associate Professor (university dependent naming)

- Reader/Associate Professor (university dependent naming)
- Professor
- Chair

Progression isn't linked to set numbers of years in post, but based on being able to demonstrate impacts across a number of different areas, and so factors that influence your progression may include:

- Research excellence – numbers of papers, grants, and research impact
- Education quality – leading on academic courses and teaching provision
- Administrative and leadership skills – taking on roles such as department head, section head, sitting on committees, systems leadership
- External recognition – involvement in professional bodies, sitting on journal editorial boards,
- Enterprise and community engagement – public engagement, engagement with widening participation programmes, involvement in prestigious conference organising committees, patents etc

Recruitment for future academic roles will always have these components in mind. During your PhD, it is therefore important to not only be aware of what might be required of you in the future, but also to actively seek out opportunities to provide you with exposure to as many of these areas as possible. Being able to not just demonstrate awareness of the academic landscape but that you have the strategic awareness to try to have enough experience to be able to talk about them, will place you in a great position to be able to compete within the academic job market.

Some of the ways that you can gain experience during your PhD that will help with your CV post completion include:

- Volunteering to sit on student committees, or to be the student representative in other forums
- Providing teaching support for courses within your department, including marking and giving lectures
- Supervising students
- Volunteering for public engagement opportunities
- Ensuring you submit abstracts for conferences
- Maximising paper outputs

- Being involved with grant submissions
- Joining and being actively involved in external discipline specific groups, such as professional bodies
- Undertaking paper reviews and, if appropriate, volunteering as a junior editor or asking to shadow a more senior journal editor
- Seeking opportunities to write blogs, be involved with podcasts, or other communication development opportunities

Not only is seeking out the above experiences useful for your future career pathway, but they also give you an opportunity to sample and identify things that you enjoy, want to know more about, and areas where you would be interested in developing further. In the long term, this aspect is also essential, as you will encounter various progression gateways that will lock you into certain routes. If you choose to become a teaching fellow, rather than a research fellow for instance, you may find it harder to find your way back to a research focussed career as your time will be taken up with teaching commitments and you will be unlikely to have enough time to support an active research portfolio.

The most important thing you can do, in addition to seeking out opportunities, is to make sure that you look at the guidance and paperwork available in order to both learn more about the system and familiarise yourself with the language. So much of your future success will be about using the right words, and speaking the right language, so you can demonstrate with clarity that you meet the expectations of those hiring. Know the boxes you need to tick, ensure that you tick them, and keep your options as open as possible, whilst finding the things that bring you joy.

CHAPTER THIRTY ONE: DEVELOPING AS A SUPERVISOR

One of the easiest development opportunities you will find access to and one of the first skills you should focus on developing alongside your research experience, is your supervision skills. This is because this skill set is something you will utilise throughout any academic career you decide to undertake, but it will also be invaluable even if you choose to leave academia. No matter where your future career lies you will need to be able to manage and supervise others, as well as train and educate on role specific information. Investing time resource into this skill will therefore never be wasted.

Now, supervision skills are composed of all kinds of aspects:

- Mentorship and coaching skills
- Communication skills
- Education and training theory
- Conflict resolution
- Emotional intelligence
- Feedback techniques
- Problem solving techniques
- Equality and diversity awareness

This can look like an intimidating list, but you're not going to develop or need all of these skills immediately, and you will need to be able to practice, as well as study, in order to develop them.

During your PhD there are likely to be multiple opportunities you can seek out in order to start developing. The first thing is to see which other students come through your department and look at volunteering to support some aspects of their placement. This may include supporting undergraduate students who are undertaking some degree level projects. Another common opportunity is to support master's placement students or even starting PhD students when you are entering your final year.

This experience can help you understand how to break down complicated information, or multi-stage techniques, in order to teach them. This in turn can help to improve your own understanding. It can also give you exposure to the fact that different students learn and work in different ways and provide you with opportunities to practice pivoting your approach, so that you switch up different styles based on the needs of your learners. Some learners will be highly visual in terms of their learning, for instance, other learners will benefit from approaches that are embedded in practical teaching rather than theoretical. It will also help you develop the communication skills you need to be able to ask questions of your students about how they learn, what kind of learning experiences they benefit from. Being able to ask the right questions, explore options, and request feedback that help you improve are components of supervision that benefit from working with a wider and diverse set of learners who are at different points in their academic journeys.

One of the other advantages of volunteering for supervision within your department is that you are likely to get to experience working both with groups of students and working one to one. This will enable you to learn a little bit about group dynamics, and how different combinations of personalities can impact on how a session you've designed and deliver can land differently. This can allow you to practice how you pivot the delivery of that session in response to how it is going, the personalities and the skill sets of the people in front of you. It can drive creativity in terms of your communication skills but also lead you to explore both your own emotional intelligence and that of your students, and to match some of your interventions to what you find.

In contrast, one to one sessions can allow you develop both a deeper understanding of the person you are working with and require you to invest in relationship building in order to build trust to maximise your time. These moments allow you to practice the use of open questions for exploring learning needs and maximising learning opportunities. They permit a coaching style approach, where it is not just about what you are asking and teaching in a directive fashion, but what your student needs and what they can bring to the experience in order to enhance both their and your learning. Once you reach a certain point with them, in terms of knowledge development, you can start to practice setting learning objectives and undertaking evaluation and giving feedback against the ones that you've set.

To help with this, there will definitely be training available within your organisation. There are higher level formal courses, but there will also be courses aimed at new supervisors that will be worth exploring. Educational theory is vast, and you are not aiming to become an expert in education at this point, unless that happens to be the area of your PhD, but understanding and being trained in some of the fundamentals will really help you expand the tools you have available. It will also enable you to undertake some self-reflection in a supported environment of what went well for you in the different education settings you've been in, and what didn't work so well. This can help you in thinking about what kind of educator you would like to be, and what your natural approaches would be. You may not always be able to use the approaches that come naturally to you, and you should be prepared to be uncomfortable in order to work with learners who have different preferences, but knowing where you might default to can be very helpful.

Finally, it's worth identifying people who you have seen supervise, and admire how they do it, and ask if they are willing to talk to you or let you shadow them. Taking time to reflect on what works for them, and whether it would work for you, can help you try out different approaches. After you've tried something new, and as opportunities become available, you should then take advantage of any chance to gain feedback on how you've done and what has worked for those you are working with. Hearing what it feels like on the other side of your supervision can help you take guided steps to get even better. Feedback is invaluable and being open to both giving and receiving it is key to any supervision relationship. Go into every conversation with a growth mindset, and value the learning you receive as a result.

CHAPTER THIRTY TWO: HOW TO WRITE YOUR FIRST GRANT

When most people hear the statement 'you should write a grant' it normally leads to a certain level of panic and definitely a sense of overwhelm. This is because the first thing that comes to mind is a major research or project grant. This isn't the kind of application that I am talking about undertaking as part of your PhD. It is possible to do this, but it's both rare and often not the right choice, as it is better to build gradually to ensure success when you are given the opportunity to lead on something big.

So, if I'm not talking about leading on a big project grant, what am I talking about? I'm talking about starting small and making the most of opportunities that come up throughout your PhD in order to make mistakes and learn from them, as well as developing your CV. The kinds of grants you are likely to be able to apply for early include:

- Conference bursaries
- Travel grants, either from professional societies or within your institution
- Small consumables funding, either from professional societies or within your institution
- Public engagement funding
- Meeting funding, to organise an event
- Placement funding, to allow you to spend time with another organisation
- Pump priming, or small project funding, either from professional societies or within your institution

There are a number of reasons to start small. First, the application forms are usually shorter, and therefore you are investing less time than you would for a larger grant if it isn't successful. Second, the sign off processes from your organisation will probably be considerably less and more straight forward. Third, they are likely to be less competitive, which means a) you are more likely to be successful but maybe even more important b) you are more likely to be able to ask for feedback if your application is not successful so you can learn how to improve your chances for future applications.

For any application type, there are some process components that undertaking small applications which will help you understand. The first of these is that it will help you understand what the processes are that your local research and development office will require you to undertake. You can take this opportunity to get to know the people who will need to be your key contacts, but also to build relationships, so you feel more comfortable asking questions and for direction. They will also be able to sign post you to courses, and guidance that will aid you in negotiating what can be a complicated landscape in the future.

A key thing to learn about when you access guidance are any restrictions on who can be involved in grant applications and in what roles. For larger grants there are usually three types of roles that feature and may be impacted by this type of local guidance:

- Primary applicant (PI): the lead on the grant who often needs to be a permanently employed member of staff for larger grants, as well as having an appropriate CV, in order to be able to be seen by funders as appropriate for leading on the proposal
- Co-applicant (Co-I): someone who is contributing to the grant and may be leading on specific work packages. They will not need to have the same level of CV as the PI but there are often restrictions on who can be named, especially if their contract of employment is not fully covered as part of the grant and the pre-existing contract does not cover the entire duration of the funding award
- Named role: this is where funding is requested as part of the application for a role, such as post doc, where the person who will be holding this role is named within the grant. This enables you to include the grant on your CV, even though not Co-I or PI, as it is assumed you will have been involved in its development

Being part of a grant as a named role helps because you will see how larger grants come together, how it changes with the different edits, how submission platforms work, and how large grant sign offs work, usually requiring sign off from: departmental leads, finance leads, and requested letters of support. One of the greatest pieces of experience to seek from these opportunities is to become familiar with how grant costing works. How do you work out how much your consumables cost? How do you work out what staff you need and for how long?

This experience is invaluable when you come to prepare your own applications.

Grant funders often present at conferences or host webinars. Even if you are not ready to start submitting yet, I would advise that you make time to attend. Funders have specific remits and gaps that sit within their funding terms. Knowing what they will fund and what they won't fund will enable you to pick the right type of funder for your work.

It is also worth seeing if they host copies of successful applications on their website, or via other means, and learn from them not only how to be successful on a similar call, but also what makes a successful grant structure in general. They will likely also have different levels of grants, and it is worth trying to understand both the written and unwritten rules by speaking to others, about which types might be most appropriate at different times in your future career. Sometimes grants are mostly about the project concept, sometimes they require a great project and a departmental track record, and things like post-doctoral fellowship applications will look at person, place and project. Knowing what's needed will be invaluable in helping develop your pitch.

Once you've done all of this groundwork, take the time to look at your CV, see what you can go for, see what helps you out most, and just get started. Know that the first few may go nowhere. Know that that's OK. Learn the lessons, get the feedback, and do everyone a little bit better than the one before. Even the best application may be unsuccessful, but you will learn something every time you make the effort to try.

CHAPTER THIRTY THREE: BECOMING COMFORTABLE WITH PUBLIC SPEAKING

It should be clear by now that conferences, and presentations at conferences, will be an important part of your academic life, both to get your work out there, but also to enable you to meet people, make connections, and achieve a successful ongoing career. Public speaking doesn't end with conferences however, although it is most commonly where you will get your start and a fair amount of practice. There will be plenty of other occasions where you might need to utilise your public speaking skills. I've needed to use mine when recording podcasts and videos, giving out awards, accepting awards, doing school and university visits, running public engagement events, and frequently within meeting and committee settings.

Not everyone is comfortable with public speaking, however, and even if you are, there will be moments or settings where you feel less at ease. No matter how comfortable you feel, there will also always be room for improvement. There will always be a new setting or a new type of presentation that you are trying out. For instance, I feel very comfortable presenting on my specialist topics, but it's taken me longer to become comfortable speaking and presenting linked to the Girlymicrobiologist blog, as that wasn't something I had not done before.

The first thing to do, in order to enhance your skills and become more comfortable, is to actively seek out opportunities to practice. Public speaking is a skill like any other, it gets better with practice, the more you do the better you will get. It can be tempting to try and duck out of presenting at departmental journal clubs, or only presenting your work when you have to, but the more regularly you do it the easier it will become. This is partly because you will gradually build up a bank of slides that you can use and combine in different ways to build the slide decks you need. Regular presenting will also stop you becoming quite so anxious, as you won't have such a large gap between experiences. This means that you can more readily tap into the fact that your previous experience was actually OK, and not as bad as you feared.

As part of seeking out these opportunities, you can try out a number of different tools that can help you practice, improve, and feel more confident. This can start out by working out what is the best approach for you to feel prepared and have access to the information you need to communicate effectively. Some options include deciding whether you want to have notes or a script to present from. It is worth bearing in mind that although these may help you in remembering what you want to say, they can prevent you from truly connecting with your audience. This is because, if you are reading from a script, you are locked into what you are going to say and can't respond to the signals that you are receiving from your audience. You can't flex the complexity of what you are presenting based on how they respond to what you are saying. Notes are better, but they can still be quite distracting for your audience. Developing enough comfort that you can present without notes or scripts is something to work towards.

An intermediate step that may enable you to become note free, is to practice your presentation ahead of time, to get feedback, practice timing, and to feel more comfortable with memorising and delivering your content without reminders. You may want to practice more if you are presenting something for the first time, or in a high-stakes setting, such as oral presentation at a conference. Whatever the reason for the presentation, consider presenting to your supervisors, your peers, and if possible, to your friends and family. Each of these audiences are likely to give you very different types of feedback, and by seeking their input you will be able to improve in a much more rounded fashion.

It is useful to know what level of preparation you need to feel comfortable. Some people benefit from rehearsing multiple times, even when they have the final version nailed down. It can be possible to rehearse too much and feel over prepared, to lose the sense of spontaneity that can really help you engage with your audience. Everyone is different, and so you will need to find the level that works for you.

Something that can also help with both your ability to connect and reducing the need to memorise facts is thinking about what to include on your slides, if you are using them. You will want to include details and facts on your slides and then talk around them, rather than just reading them verbatim. You may want to seat this additional information in stories and storytelling, so it enhances your audience connection. Human beings tend to respond to storytelling and it can help provide your audience with additional context, which will help them remember key pieces of information as you move through your talk. Eventually, you will develop the confidence to share more and more of yourself as you speak, which will only work to make your ability to connect with your audience better.

One aspect that many people forget about when they practice, is non-verbal communication. Most people focus on the slides and associated content and forget about the presentation aspect. This is something that it can be harder to get detailed feedback on, but there are techniques that can help with this. One that is easily accessible to most people is to set up your mobile phone and record yourself giving a talk, whether a real one or a practice session. You can then watch it back and reflect on how you communicate, both in terms of verbal and non-verbal communication. Do you move a lot when you speak? Do you use your arms and gestures to emphasise what you are saying? Do you do this too much, too little, or about right? Do you unconsciously use filler words or sounds? Do you say umm or like me say 'actually' far too much. Do you make eye contact? Do you speak at the right volume? As much as it can feel cringe worthy, undertaking this type of exercise and actively working on what you see can be very helpful in improving how you come across.

It is OK to feel nervous about public speaking. Anxiety is normal; it just shouldn't stop you. Identify what makes you nervous and take active steps to prepare and manage that stress. Remember, hardly anyone recalls the bad talks they've been to. If they do, they remember the content not the speaker, and no one remembers after more than a few weeks. Audiences remember the brilliant and inspiring. The novel and the authentic. So, aim high, what is the worst that can happen?

CHAPTER THIRTY FOUR: EMBEDDING YOUR 360° DEVELOPMENT

So far, we've covered some key areas that you will be able to access and gain from specific experience linked to your PhD, and why you need to maintain an approach that is broad enough to enable you to meet academic progression criteria. It is worth bearing in mind that there are plenty of areas of development, commonly known as soft skills, that will aid in your long-term prospects, both within and outside of academia.

These soft skills fall broadly within the following categories:

- Communication skills
- Leadership and influencing skills
- Teamworking skills
- Conflict management and assertiveness skills
- Project and time management skills
- Stress management skills
- Analysis skills
- Self-assessment and reflection skills

Almost all universities will have both a programme of teaching sessions that you can tap into to actively work on developing these skills, not least of all because they will benefit your PhD as well as your ongoing career. They will often also have a self-assessment tool, which I would recommend you utilise at least every 6 months to see how far you have developed, but also to aid in identification of any development gaps. It is worth splitting these self-assessments into knowledge, skills and behaviours. This means that you can identify where you need to tap into courses to increase your knowledge. Where you need to identify opportunities to apply that knowledge and thus increase the associated skills, and where you can utilise reflection to change your practice linked with the area. If your university doesn't provide these kinds of skills, then they are available from other sources on the web, and you can always keep an eye on the Girlymicrobiologist.com website for useful links.

It is important to not just focus on the things that come easily, and to be aware of the breadth of development available under each heading. For instance, if you think of improving your communication skills, you should consider not just presentation and grant/thesis writing skill i.e. the things you will encounter and are embedded as part of your PhD work. Take every chance to experience the parts that are less linked to your research, such as writing lay summaries, or public information leaflets. Take every chance to present, small or large, no matter how terrified you are, and every opportunity to copy edit someone else's grant or paper. All of it will enable you to see how other people communicate and find new ideas for things you like or get you to put your research dissemination in a new way to a different audience. The only way you get better at any of these topics is by putting in the hours, there are no short cuts. It is always better to grow organically, rather than waiting until you have a specific need.

One of the areas that I haven't covered so much is leadership. It can often feel challenging to develop leadership skills when you don't consider yourself to be in a leadership position. The thing is, we often think of leadership in a hierarchical sense, with leaders being in a position of authority. That type of leadership certainly does exist, but there are plenty of examples where leadership can be demonstrated and experienced that aren't through formal structures. This is called informal leadership, and you can readily demonstrate it through simple acts, such as taking responsibility for organising the monthly departmental journal club or even overseeing the coffee rota. It is all about the application of the skill set rather than the size or impact of the task. For leadership it is especially important to consider your full experiences, both in and out of work, as there are likely to be many examples you can utilise outside of your academic setting.

All of which brings me onto the reflection that I've talked so much about in this book, but I haven't really discussed how you undertake it in a systematic fashion. Self-reflection is a slightly different process to the self-assessment you will undertake linked to knowledge, skills and behaviours. It is more linked to setting aside time to think about events that have happened, explore how they went and how they could go differently if they were to happen again, and what your learning is linked to that reflection. Again, there are several different tools available to help you, and you will probably want to explore a number of them to find the one you like best.

I tend to use the 5 R's, as it works for the way I think, and it includes the following stages:

- Reporting of the experience and any context linked to it
- Responding to the experience (observations, feelings, thoughts, etc.)
- Relating the experience to knowledge and skills you already have
- Reasoning about the significant factors/theory that help you to explain what happened
- Reconstructing your practice by planning future actions and learning linked to if you were to encounter the experience again in the future

Getting into the habit of being self-aware enough to undertake both self-assessment of your knowledge, skills and behaviours, and regular self-reflection to inform your learning and development decisions, will benefit you life long, both in work, but also in life. It is too easy to drift through your career without being decisive or directional in the development of these more generic skill sets. It is also easy to think that you can attend a single course, or training event, and that it alone will tick the box needed for your CV. Although it is true that being able to list activities undertaken will help you to gain roles or complete an application form, there is a difference in a mindset that focusses on box ticking, versus one that focusses on true growth and development.

Entering every phase of your career with a mindset that embraces growth and true development will enable you to be dynamic and flexible as new opportunities present themselves and is also a satisfying way to approach the exciting situations you will find yourself in throughout your career. Learning for the joy of learning every day.

CHAPTER THIRTY FIVE: LEARNING TO HANDLE FAILURE

One of the skills that probably wasn't on your list anywhere to develop was your ability to handle and process failure. This may seem something that is strange to talk about in a book about how to achieve a PhD, but handling failure is a key and oft undiscussed part of working in academia. It always struck me as pretty ironic that academia takes a whole workforce of people who have often never failed an exam and pride themselves in academic accomplishment and put them in a landscape where failure is a fact of life. It is often said that only 20% of grants are successful, which is tough when for quite a few years your ongoing employment will rely upon them. On top of this rejection will be a regular feature, be it for papers, conference submissions, or promotion. Despite this, no one ever talks about the fact that the ability to manage your response to these moments is a skill in and of itself. Something that needs to be managed, developed, and actively worked upon.

We are taught that failure is a bad thing, but I've come to believe that the opposite is in fact true. Each failure is a learning opportunity. Each failure is a moment where we can choose to grow. Learning to see these moments in a different way and how to handle them will be a crucial part of your journey if you choose to stay within an academic career. You will learn more from each failure than you will from each success, and so failure is often experienced more at each gateway, and especially when you are transitioning between phases of your career. It often indicates that change and improvement is on its way, and hopefully, that good things will be around the corner.

Let's start by being honest. Failure hurts. It does. There's no way around it. If it didn't hurt so much most of us wouldn't fear it. I think, however, that the reason it hurts as much as it does is because it forces us to have a look in the mirror and reassess, often with increased clarity. It forces introspection upon us, and that can be a challenging thing. It is particularly hard as no one really talks about it and so it can feel like you are the only one going through it, but we all fail, I fail all the time. Now sometimes those failures are big and sometimes they are small and minor, like not having a conversation well. I wasted a lot of time at the start of my career by trying to be perfect and consequently I feel

I didn't maximise the learning in those first few years. If I discovered an error I quickly (and safely) corrected it, but I had such anxiety over it I didn't really reflect on it, I wanted to fix it and move on.

Failure is inevitable however, it's a key part of the learning process, and the sooner we embrace that inevitability, the better placed we will be to deal with it when it arrives. Developing coping strategies and knowing yourself enough to manage your response is key. One way to do this is to think about being strategic in your approach. For instance, you may want to always ensure that you have at least two grant applications in at any one time. Therefore, if grant A is rejected, you can have hope that grant B will succeed.

The other thing is understanding how to manage yourself. Rather than being in denial that failure will happen you need to allow yourself to feel and process the emotions associated with it, so you can find a way through and move on. Allow yourself an indulgent short grieving period for failure. That's it. After that move to a more forward focused place. What's next? What have you learnt? Try to move through the emotional aspects and allow your logical brain to kick in. Use that new headspace to undertake a true review, there's always something that can be learnt. Be that based on feedback you've received, be that based on how you've handled either the initial experience or your response to it. You will always be in a position to take onboard more knowledge linked to the strategic landscape you are working in; which will enable you to do better next time. Being open to this learning is what moves failure iteratively towards success.

One main thing to evaluate when a 'no' is a 'not for us' – taking yourself out of the mix. Context is key. Without it, you can't truly get to a place where you can understand feedback. There is, for instance, a big difference between a no and a not for us. I know the outcome is the same, but the process of moving forward is different. If something is 'not for us' it feels different. A flat 'no' can feel like a value judgement. It can feel like the idea/work is bad. A 'not for us' doesn't feel the same. It means that the drivers and vision of the people who are assessing don't align with your proposal, and the learning is to do a better job of matching your concepts with the remit of who you may submit to in the future. This type of rejection is actually an opportunity, an opportunity to find someone who better aligns with where you want to be. Think of it as an opportunity to open a different set of doors.

The other technique that can help is to focus on what you can control. There is so much within the academic landscape that you can't control. That said, in the process, there is so much that you can control. You can control your approach, who you are submitting to, what your aspirations for the work are, and how you balance that with other pieces of work that you have in process. One way to develop and maintain a sense of control is to understand there is never a single route to getting things done. There are always multiple ways to approach any aspiration and once you acknowledge this, you can make sure you include some of these alternatives in your planning.

Another component of this is to make sure that 'the plan' is rooted in realism, in both approach and time scale. There is nothing more disheartening than having a plan/approach that fails due to a lack of research/understanding. This is where your baseline skills as a researcher will come into their own. No matter the task, take the time to familiarise yourself with the barriers and options to ensure your plan is up to scratch. Sometimes, the dream itself is not enough. Running head-on at goal can, at times, be both painful and exhausting. When this becomes overwhelming, it's sometimes better to choose to come at things sideways or progress associated goals for a while. For instance, if that paper has been rejected for the 4th time, it might be time to write a blog post on it and use that as a different opportunity to think about the core message.

When it all becomes too much, press the reset button and decide whether it's the direction that you still want to travel in. Take a moment to return to your why. Despite all of these thoughts about how to manage rejection and carry on, I want to make clear that it is also OK to think about quitting. This sounds a bit strange doesn't it, after all, in academia we don't quit. Except we do. Part of our growth is being able to reexamine our work, be that an experiment, paper, or project in light of new information. When you get rejections, then it is important to decide whether someone has spotted a fundamental flaw that you just can't fix or takes the work in a direction you just don't want to follow. This isn't encouragement to throw the baby out with the bath water, but an acknowledgement that there are times when the right decision is to pause or discard a piece of work and that it's important to acknowledge that as part of our processing.

Once you've decided that you are still invested or that the piece of work you are doing still has value, to you or others, then it's important to remind yourself of how far you've come. It will always be further than you think. This is easier if you had a plan when starting out, but even if not, you can spend 10 minutes just listing all the steps you have proactively taken in moving towards your goal. Listing your rejections and the learning from them is a key part of this evaluation process. Putting everything down in one place may enable you to see opportunities you might have missed or help develop your plan B and C options further. I would advocate doing this regularly, even in the absence of rejections, but it can be a particularly useful re-centering process when things feel hard.

Finally, if you've decided that what you are undertaking still matches your why, and that it is not flawed enough to walk away from, the only thing to do is to suck it up, acknowledge your feelings and get on with it. Keep the faith, both in the work and yourself, and go all in despite how hard it can feel. Have a plan and take a single step at a time, until, before you know it, you've reached your destination. Anything worthwhile is worth the effort, and future you will thank past you for your persistence and determination. Have a hard conversation with yourself and just keep going. I promise the payoff will be worth it.

CHAPTER THIRTY SIX: CHOOSING YOUR NEXT CAREER STEPS

When you finish any big piece of career development it is both joyous and, for me, confusing. You have been running head long towards a goal for years, laser focussed on crossing that finish line. If, like me, you focus so much on the target you forget to think about what comes next, the end can be quite jarring. So, I think it's actually important to build in time to review throughout the process, if possible, but definitely at the end. Which aspects did you really enjoy and would like to ensure you include as a priority in any future career planning? Which bits did you not enjoy? Can the bits you didn't enjoy be avoided, or reduced by making decisions linked to next steps? Bearing in mind we all have bits of any job we don't adore. If the bits you dislike are a feature of academia, then maybe also think more widely about where your disciplinary interests might fit.

Another thing that it is worth doing, is really taking some time to map and focus on your skill gaps. The great thing about entering a different career phase it that it is an opportunity to really re-invent yourself and reset. The next thing you do, academia wise, after a PhD might be pretty different. Choosing a post doc is an opportunity to take all you've experienced during your PhD and use it make a more informed decision about your future. It may be that you, for example, had never had the opportunity to undertake bioinformatics before your third year, and now it really interests and inspires you. What skills would you need to develop to have this as a more dominant feature in your career? What further experience do you need to make you competitive in the job market? Then use this reflection to make informed choices when you are developing your next steps.

The natural consequence of identifying your skill gaps is an acceptance that you will need to be prepared for the studying and learning to continue even when your PhD comes to an end. You reach the end of your PhD and most of us say that's it, we are never studying again. Then, within a fairly short time, reality makes a liar of us all. If you want an academic career, then the studying will continue. There will be a need to become a better educator, as well as researcher, to ensure you remain competitive in the job market. There are always new techniques and specialist skills to pick up, and I would make a plea that we could all do with spending some time on developing our communication skills. I'm talking everything from grant writing skills, to media training and public engagement skills. No matter how little you think you need some of these things, you will always need them more than you predict. The added bonus is that they will also beneficially impact on other parts of your work, for instance things like public engagement skills make your general presentation skills better.

In light of these ongoing requirements, it can be useful to take some time to focus on you and review your personal priorities as you reach the end of your PhD. Reflection is always worth it, but as you may have been working towards something for a period of years whilst life went on around you it is a good idea to seize this moment to truly invest in yourself and take some active reflection time. Giving yourself some time to decide what now holds meaning for you, what work life balance looks like for you, and what your priorities are, will mean you maintain yourself as well as your career along the way.

Hopefully this book will mean that you have the best PhD experience possible, but if it didn't go so well, it can be tempting to walk away from everything linked to what you've just completed, into the sunset, and never look back. Some people have great PhD experiences, some have awful ones, and most people have a time of both highs and lows. No matter how tempting it is to close the door on this chapter of your life this is my plea to you to consider maintaining those links. You will have spent years working in an environment where you will have invested in networks, relationships and learning. Utilising that foundation, even if not all of it, to support your next steps is one of the best things that can come out of your PhD. It doesn't have to be via your supervisor, but through the peers you bonded with, or even other academics you encountered along the way. Invest a little in making sure that you don't lose the things you have already put a lot of energy into when you start to move into something new.

Now, having talked about maintaining the old, we all know people who've clung so tightly to where they've come from that they never really move forward. This is also not great. You're entering a new phase, and you can't truly maximise on the potential of that if you carry over too much of where you've been. If you want to continue to thrive, this is the time to expand and find your new tribe. This can be an intimidating time, but there are often routes out there within your organisation that really support you in doing this. I would advocate that, during any career transition phase, it is worth taking some time to see if you can find a mentor or get access to coaching, in order to help you through the reflection and to maximise the opportunity.

Coming out of something, like a PhD, where your focus has had to be on a single very defined goal, it can be tempting to approach the next phase of your career in the same way. I don't think it hurts to have focus, to have your list of gaps to address, and the things you've identified that you want to include and prioritise. I also want to suggest that you might want to consciously keep the non-subject specific aspects of even your PhD broad to ensure that you maximise your opportunities to try and experience a breadth of options. Not just to help inform future decision making, but also because you can't progress on the basis of one area of interest alone.

You may be an amazing researcher, but you also need to know how to communicate your research. You may be a wonderful teacher, but you also need to develop your strategic awareness skills in order to understand how best to navigate the system you find yourself in. Be aware of your future career needs and make sure you don't close doors without realising it by failing to maintain and grow across development areas and know how much these areas cross support each other to make you the best academic you can be.

That isn't to say that your only option at the end of your PhD is to stay in academia. There are plenty of places outside of universities that would be keen to offer you a position, from government departments to private industry. By keeping your foundation broad, you will also enable you to pivot as part of your next steps. So much of what that next step looks like will depend upon why you undertook a PhD in the first place. You should also bear in mind that it is OK to try out living in the academic landscape, thinking it was your dream, and subsequently decide that it's not for you once you have come face to face with the reality of what it offers. Whatever your choice, it is valid, just make sure it is thought out and the best and most informed choice for you.

Whatever choice you make, just be aware that you will encounter forks in the road, and that the pathway sold to you may not be as direct as you were told it was. You will encounter unexpected opportunities, barriers that you need to traverse around, and unexpected diversions along the way. In the moment you may fail to see either the learning or the joy of these diversions, but you will often find, looking back, that these diversions and deviations end up providing the experiences and opportunities where you learn most about yourself, or gain the most in terms of career progression. Being open to the less travelled path can reap unexpected rewards. Being open minded when presented with choices, and sometimes overlooking short term gain, can have great career benefits in the long term.

Sometimes this flexibility is also about allowing yourself to choose to prioritise your personal priorities at times over career ones. It can feel like, if you are making a choice, it is a permanent closing of a door but more often than not it is a choice you are making for right now based on what works for you. Being mindful of when choices are permanent or for 'right now' can be really helpful in evaluating next moves. Also, knowing that your choices are about you and what's right for your life, and not listening too much to outside distractions can be helpful. It may be right for you to move into industry, to step back from clinical, to move into strategy or policy, only you can judge. There can be perceived judgement linked to leaving a standard academic path, but career paths are so much more diverse and flexible than they used to be, and so we should not just accept but embrace the freedom that creates.

It can be easy to become a passenger in the early stages of your career, and then once you've established yourself enough to know who you are you've travelled down a path that takes time to re-set. Being able to communicate your values, beliefs and core vision, is essential in so many different interactions, be they in your personal or professional life. Doing this well means you are less likely to be swayed or worse mis-labelled, leading you to end up somewhere that is out of alignment with who you are and where you want to be. This path leads to unhappiness and real issues with career satisfaction and fulfilment. Don't be a passenger in someone else's story, or an imitation of someone else's aspirations, work hard to ensure you are the leading character in your own life. That is the path to real satisfaction in your career and supports you finding the happiness you deserve in your day-to-day life.

CHAPTER THIRTY SEVEN: POSITIONING YOURSELF FOR SUCCESS

We all have moments of high and low confidence. One of the things that I've learnt is how important it is to notice and acknowledge whatever period you're in, but not let it impact on activity, as how you're feeling personally does not really alter your chances of success on any given thing, after all success is linked to factors other than your mood. It is all too easy to decide not to apply for grants or other things if you are feeling underconfident. It is also possible to be too comfortable and therefore miss out on applying because you feel a lack of urgency. The thing is, the most important thing, for both your CV and your development is consistency. You won't get better at writing grants, papers etc if you aren't doing it, so even if you don't 'need' to do it as you have funding that doesn't mean that you shouldn't. You may just choose to apply for a public engagement or development grant instead, but you should still do it.

One thing that will impact your career most are the connections and networks you build during your PhD. It is through these connections you will gain invites and opportunities. More than just that though, it is where you will find your mentors and the people you can link into for guidance and advice. So much of a career in academia is based on who you know and who you collaborate with. The problem is making those connections and getting to know people, especially in the early part of your career, often requires taking the plunge and being the one to open a conversion with someone you've never met.

Luckily there are so many different ways to meet people and form connections these days, although the classic way of meeting people at conferences is still a great way to meet a lot of people in a period of days rather than building up remote links over months. With this in mind there are some moments and set ups at conferences when it is easier to start a conversation than others. There is always the chance that the person next to you in an interesting session will strike up a conversation to help them process what they've heard but in general they will be doing the same as you, ducking into and out of sessions that trigger their fancy, meaning they will be you focused on what comes next not starting a chat.

I find, however, there are two key moments when people are available for the cold start up conversation. The first is at food breaks/receptions. During these moments there will be people who are there solo and also looking to develop their networks. I find the best thing to do in these situations is to get there early. There are always a limited number of tables where people can put down drinks, if you can find one and hold a place then people will effectively come to you. If this fails and there are no tables, just being close to the source of the refreshments often does the same job. Food and drink are great removers of hierarchy and being somewhere visible means that those in a similar position to you will be able to see you and hopefully will head your way. Worst case you make some small talk to the group that comes to your table, and you can politely extricate yourself if it all feels too weird by saying you're popping to get another drink.

The other place where people will be desperate to speak to you is during poster sessions. So many people will be waiting at their posters for an hour in the desperate hope that someone will come and show an interest. This can shortcut some of the small talk you might otherwise need to make. It also enables you to know whether you are making a connection with a peer or whether you are connecting with a potential mentor/future employer. It is often a great time to make connections/exchange contact details, so keep some business cards handy.

Social media platforms have opened up a whole new way to make connections and maintain relationships, there are great pros to this, but also some words of warning. The first thing to do is to think about which platforms you wish to use, are used frequently within your academic discipline, and what the USP you want to present would be. I would encourage you to set up social media early on in your PhD to help with linking and dissemination. I would choose a profile name that links in strongly to that USP and one that you will maintain throughout your academic career. I would be clear that the profile states that all the opinions stated are your own and not linked to your employer. For this reason, I would also set up new accounts that you use for professional, public, communication, rather than utilising personal ones you already have in place. You will probably want to keep your own personal profiles as private rather than public, and it is helpful to delineate between the two.

When thinking about which platforms you wish to set up on, you should consider platforms that are more linked with professional activities, such as LinkedIn. You should also think about whether you have the skills and want to invest the time in producing content for platforms that are more video based, such as TikTok and YouTube. It is also worth considering that social media platforms rise and fall, therefore you will need to a) maintain awareness of where to invest your time and b) where the kind of content you wish to produce will fit best. For instance, I am happy to sit and write on a Sunday morning in my pyjamas, but I'm not prepared to film a video, and so my content tends to be via a blog than a vlog. It is also worth knowing that growing any kind of following takes time and energy. You will need to be present to respond frequently and post/interact on a regular basis. So, consider what you will be able to manage in terms of time commitments, and what the payoff will be.

Once you are set up then you can utilise all of the social media networking options both within and outside of conferences. These days every conference/meeting has a hashtag. By following this hashtag, you can find people who are interested in the same things as you, people who are in the same sessions or who even have shared connections. In many ways it's an improved version of doing the poster walk. Not only does this give you a conversational in, but also by posting yourself linked to the thread, before you ever meet in person, it allows you to have a low stakes initial introduction. You can also find people that you primarily know online in order to strengthen your networks by getting to know each other better. It gives you the chance to arrange collaboration events, like podcast recordings, when you happen to be in the same place for a limited time. Both of these can obviously be done by email but can be much easier to arrange when at an event, when you suddenly have half an hour free. Especially at big conferences you could wander the halls for 4 days and not meet anyone you know, this way you can make the most of every second.

Beyond networking, one other skill you need to practice is having the confidence to throw your hat into the ring, even if you aren't sure that you are ready or prepared. Not only is applying to sit on committees, or groups a good way of meeting people and broadening your skill sets, you often don't know where these roles and opportunities will lead you. It is often said that readiness is a state of mind rather than linked to a specific skill set. Practice makes perfect, and you won't always succeed in the moment, but the experience gained will always stand you in good stead.

Stepping up to be a part of these meetings can still be nerve wracking, even I still get insecure when going into high stakes meetings. You can't necessarily control the nerves that you feel, but there are things that you can do to help. The first of which is to make sure you understand your role in the room, are you there to help make decisions, are you there to advise, are you there to take tasks and make things happen? Once you understand your role, then you will want to understand the role of the wider committee and where it sits within the landscape it works within. Where does the committee you are sitting on report into? Does anyone report into it? Does it have a terms of reference which lays out who else sits on the committee and their roles? All of these pieces of information can help you understand what is expected of you and the committee or meeting you are attending.

Once you know what the expectations are you can focus on process, which can help you feel prepared. This one is all about getting documentation, like previous agendas if available, and other supporting information. Reading through these will help you get a feel for what being in the room is like. It gives you time to reflect on what you could bring to the table. What is it that you can offer? Where were you successful in your application to join, or why were you invited? Know there is a reason you are in the room and focus on the why of that.

The other thing that you can do, which will also help with your networking, is to reach out to other people who will be in attendance. This could be someone else who is attending that you know or are aware of. It could also be that you speak to the Chair or the Deputy Chair, so that the first time you meet them isn't in the meeting itself. It can take courage to bring your whole self into a new space, but it is by leading with authenticity that you will make the largest impact. Becoming familiar enough that you can be fully yourself within the room is an important step in self-facilitation to enable you to perform at your best.

The truth of long-term success is that it requires you to place yourself in positions where you can maximise the opportunities that come your way. Having awareness of the requirements for your academic progression. Making connections, having a strategic vision, and a plan, will all help deliver on and enhance your existing academic portfolio. You can't be successful on your own, so prioritise finding your people, finding your team, and then work together so that you can make your dreams and aspirations a reality.

CHAPTER THIRTY EIGHT: COMMUNICATING WITH NON-ACADEMICS

It is completely normal to focus on building your communication skills to enable you to speak to your peers, and academics within your field. This is the reason that this book has focussed a lot on how to prepare papers and presentations. There is another audience, however, that it is becoming increasingly important to consider as part of your communication and dissemination options, one that may require you to develop and practice your communication skills in a different way, that audience is the general public.

Why should you care about speaking to non-academics? There are a number of reasons, with the first being that if you are funded by a research grant, that research funding has often come from a research council or other funder where their money has come from either public donations, or taxpayer contributions. This means that at the end of the day, our final employer is actually the general public, and you should therefore feel that you have a duty to let them know what you have been doing with their money.

Another reason why you should want to speak to non-academics is that it's a way to maximise the impact of your work. Many aspects of academic research are of interest to the public, whether you are working on soldier graffiti from World War Two or a disease resistant crop variant. Now, the public may be interested in different ways, for the first you might want to find the relatives of the soldiers involved or see if a book would be interesting to the wider populace, for the second you might wish to have conversations to see if there would be resistance or perceived barriers to implementation of the crop as part of the wider food chain. Knowing how and when it might be helpful, both for your work and its reception, to engage the public is a skill that is worth developing to maximise your impact across your career journey.

There will also be times when you want to speak to the public that isn't directly linked to dissemination of your work. This is often more linked to your role within academia. I clearly remember the university student who came to speak to my class when I was in primary school.

He was great, he was engaging, he didn't look anything like me. Not that he needed to, I didn't really even think about that at the time. When you ask most people what a scientist looks like, they will draw a picture of a man. If you ask most people what a professor looks like, they will draw a picture of an old man. Although I didn't think about the fact that the PhD student didn't look anything like me, I wonder how much more I would have been inspired if they had.

All of us have something different to offer, drawn from what makes us unique. Giving light to that uniqueness, and demonstrating that you can be successful within academia, irrespective of factors such as chronic illness, gender, social background, race, disability or who you choose to love, is a powerful message for the future no matter what the audience you are speaking to. Learning how to speak not just about your chosen discipline, but to do so with authenticity will deepen your connection with those you are communicating with and enhance the impact of what you are trying to achieve. Showing that who you are should never be a barrier to success is a message that will never stop needing to be told.

There are ways that learning how to do this better can even enhance your career. Many research funders these days will require you to write things like lay (written for people who are not experts) abstracts as part of any grant funding application. There are funders that will require you to have members of the public on any project groups, and still others that will have lay members of the public on interview committees for fellowship and large project funding. When you are looking at trying out for grant funding, there are also likely to be public engagement grants that will not only be helpful practice for application experience but also support your research dissemination costs.

When writing for a non-expert audience there are a few things you might want to consider:

- The average UK reading age in 2024 was between 9 and 11 years of age, and so word choice needs to match this and be accessible
- What are your trying to communicate and why
- Who will your audience be comprised of
- How long will you have your audience, often short and snappy is better
- Are slides the best way, or will people respond more to you

connecting and just describing your content

- Be aware of using abbreviation, most people won't understand them, and they are an unnecessary barrier
- What is the one message you would like people to take away

There are plenty of ways to gain experience and practice how you will put together different types of communication. There are engagement schemes, such as I'm a Scientist Get Me Out of Here, run by the Wellcome Trust and the National Humanities Centre Fellow Forum, that will enable you to get some experience in a supported and structured setting. There are also schemes that support pairing academics with schools, so that you can list what you are happy to talk about and where you are prepared to travel to, and they will match you up. Universities will also have outreach programmes and widening participation schemes that you can take the opportunity to support. All of this is before you think about reaching out to charities and special interest groups, who might be very excited to have you come and speak to them about your area of research interest.

Not only should we want to give back as academics to those that help pay our salaries, but undertaking this kind of work helps us and our research to be better and have more impact. You will become a much better educator if you become used to altering your pitch based on your audience, or your content based on the expertise in the room. You will become a much better leader and supervisor if you become more comfortable with sharing aspects of yourself, and how to do that in a way that is effective without putting you outside your comfort zone. Public engagement opens up new funding avenues and opportunities, as well as supporting the development of your CV. So, dive in and give it a try, everybody wins.

CHAPTER THIRTY NINE: MARKETING YOURSELF AND YOUR UNIQUE SELLING POINTS

The truth is, if you don't define yourself, you will be defined by other people. It is natural for human beings to want to put each other into boxes, that's how we process and see the world, but you need to step up and choose which boxes are right for you and not be scared if they are perceived as different or unusual. Knowing how to communicate who you are, your unique selling points, and almost developing your own brand, can also help others understand and support you.

In Chapter 4, I wrote about developing your elevator pitch to help with applying for your doctoral programme, but at the point you are finishing that PhD, it is a good time to revisit both your elevator pitch, and more importantly your USP, in order to decide whether it has changed and what it is that now matters to you most. You will want to include all of your learning, both about your topic but also about yourself, into your new revised USP, so that you have something that serves the next phase of your career.

Just a reminder, the three questions that you need to be addressing are:

- Who you are? – based on your core values
- Where you are now? – linked to your current interests and experiences
- Where are you interested in getting to and why?

You may want to consider some of the below prompts for what you might have experienced during your PhD programme and that you might want to think about for inclusion:

- Knowledge (technique, setting or organism)
- Access (organism, patients, research equipment)
- Support (mentorship, peer-peer)
- Collaboration (shared goals, shared research, shared implementation)

Once you have begun the process of crystalising and defining yourself, you can start the process of making sure that it is clearly embedded in all you do, whether that's within your social media profiles, or in making your next career steps.

Think about simple things, such as including key roles you hold as part of your email signature, as well as your role title. If you haven't set up a LinkedIn account, now is the time to do it. Use your crafted USP statement to fill in the 'about yourself' section, so that who you are is up front for everyone to see. Then think carefully about who you reach out and connect with. Make sure you're making connection decisions on the basis of the professional identity you have defined, rather than treating it as a personal connection tool for friends.

Consider what other platforms exist that will enable you to build a profile, that will help you in making connections, either for collaboration or future role opportunities. Do some research before you set up your profile, make sure you know what kind of description will enable you to find the right connections, and check out the profiles of others to choose things that make them stand out and include in your own design process. Think about making sure you choose a photo of yourself rather than a generic picture or a cat, as this will make it easier for people to find you at conferences, and mean people are more likely to connect with you as they are less likely to believe you to be a bot.

See whether your platforms will allow you to cross post. Try to harmonise your IDs across platforms, so that you strengthen your ID and brand. Consider what types of posts should be used for each and do some research about the frequency of posting required. For instance, you probably need to post three times a week, currently, for LinkedIn, whereas you need to try and post daily on platforms like Instagram.

Undertake some research about how tags and hashtags will work on your platforms of choice and think about keeping a list that you will search for to find similar posts and utilise in your sharing. You will likely need to modify these based on the audience you are trying to reach on different platforms, but trying to be consistent will enable you to grow a following over time and also keep you tied to your central messaging linked to how you've decided to define yourself.

It's not just about social media, however, now is the time to think about setting up your academic website that will host links to your papers, talks that you've presented, posters that you've created, alongside public engagement content. This should be designed in a way that is effectively an easy to navigate graphical CV. This will be something you can grow alongside your career but will give you a central place where you can speak directly to those who are interested in your work, be they academics or a wider audience. It also becomes really helpful over time to have this central repository, as over the years you will forget where the links to podcast X or video Y are and having them easily accessible is a useful resource for you as the years roll on. It may feel sparse at the start but trust me it won't be that way for long.

One of my biggest tips for marketing yourself is to invest in getting some business cards printed, even if you have to pay to have them printed yourself. It adds an air of professionalism, and if you design your own, as you are paying, you can make sure they align with your USP. Always keep some to hand as it means you have something easy to hand out or pin to posters if you want others to get in touch. If you take the time to make them distinct, they also help make you memorable. If you have your own website and social media profiles, include these, so that you are signposting to your content and what you have to offer.

You don't have to be a marketing expert to pick up some of these activities and make them effective. As an academic, no one expects marketing and self-promotion to be your strength. To be honest it can be a bit uncomfortable, but this is the world we live and work in if we're trying to expand our impact and maximise the opportunities available moving forward. Like so much in your career, you can get so much more out of just a little inputted resource, if you do it in a well planned and thought-out way. Invest some time, and perhaps a little money, into yourself to enable you to put your best foot forward and continue to reap the rewards for years to come. When you get set up, drop me a note, I'm Girlymicro just about everywhere. We can amplify each other's signals.

CHAPTER FORTY: PAYING IT FORWARD

For a long time, academics have been considered to be 'other', to work in ivory towers that keep them distant from the rest of society. Clever people who focus on things that don't impact the real world. This also means that a lot of people can't see themselves as being given access, or becoming part of that academic world, meaning that the kinds of people who go on to become academics don't necessarily reflect the rest of society. This matters, as it means that the people who are coming up with the questions, and directing knowledge gained, are not necessarily coming up with the best ones. They will be asking questions that matter for the vision of the world that they experience, but the real questions that need to be the focus may just be ones they don't see and therefore can't consider. If we want the best out of academia, if we want the best out of research, then those people undertaking that research need to look like, and represent, all of the people from the wider society that research is undertaken within.

This book came out of an increasing awareness that this isn't the case. Academia doesn't work for all people, because all people are not represented within it. Increasingly, because of the cost of tuition and other fees, accessing academic careers is becoming even more requiring of privilege. Privilege in terms of the money to undertake degrees, privilege in terms of being able to see yourself within the academic landscape, and privilege in terms of access to the kind of information that will allow you to even navigate the process to get onto PhD programmes to start with. Access is limited by resource, both in terms of money and knowledge.

Now, I can't do much directly about access to money, although I hope this book gives some starter information linked to applying for funding that might help. What I can do something about is trying to get information out there so that you don't need to know someone who has already done a PhD, or already has an academic career, to get access to the information about how to get onto a PhD programme, or enable you to find out enough information about what it's like and what is expected, for you to decide whether it is the right choice for you.

Those of you reading this book who take the next steps or speak to other people who are thinking about whether a PhD is the right step for them, this book aims to level the playing field. It is my attempt to pay it forward, to benefit those that will come after me, and to share what I have learnt along the way. To mean that the world of academia better represents the real world it should serve.

The thing is this shouldn't stop with me. The Girlymicrobiologist blog is all about building community, community where we support and lift each other up, where we pay it forward to leave the landscape better than how we found it. My hope is that if you find this book helpful you will also join me in trying to help others. In taking every opportunity when we open doors to keep them open, rather than closing them behind us. The academic landscape will change; you will learn things that I don't know. My hope is that you will also decide to take steps to pay what you learn forward, to share the knowledge held in this book, but also the knowledge that you gain when you are going through this experience.

I hope that you will find ways to reach people who might not always have access to it by any other means. To find a way to reach people that I cannot reach, and to make sure that sharing doesn't stop with you, by also talking to them about why they should continue the chain. At the end of the day this is all a choice, and one that we need to make and actively put resource into in order to make the whole system better.

So, choose.

Choose to share what you learn.

Choose to stand tall, proud of who you are and where you've come from, so that others who follow don't only see the view of a 'traditional' academic.

Choose to help others, even if you may never meet them or know their name.

Be visible. Be seen. Be the change.

TOP TIPS FOR FUTURE SUCCESS

Finishing a PhD is such an exciting time, you have so many routes open to you, so many choices yet to make, all of which will help you transition into a fulfilling onward career. Choice can sometimes be intimidating however, and so here are some final top tips to help you navigate towards your future.

Don't focus purely on academic skills to the exclusion of your other skill sets

Of course, a PhD is an academic training programme, but succeeding in an academic career is about so much more than research skills, so put some time into thinking about what other skills and experiences you need to develop. Don't lose track of these and focus purely on ticking off your research boxes. When it comes to being successful in your next job interview, in academia or not, it is these skills that will often be the difference between a yes or a no, as everyone will be coming with a similar academic CV.

Ensure you remember the importance of people in your journey

When you reach the end of any phase in your life, it can be tempting to close the door and move on, whether the experience has been good or not so great. You can become so focussed on the future, and be so keen to move on, that you forget to maintain your previous relationships. Academia is a relatively small and niche world however, and so it is important to be aware of how you are moving on. Repair relationships that have suffered because of stress, maintain connections that have supported you along the way, as well as looking to create new ones. Relationships and people will be a constant feature if you are to be successful moving forward.

Embrace every opportunity, even if you are unsure where it will lead

With so many choices and opportunities in front of you, it can be hard to know which ones to follow up. Being open to everything offered to you, even if you don't say yes to everything all at once, will stand you in good stead, as you won't always be able to predict where things will lead. Some of the things I've done, that have yielded the most satisfying results or opened the most doors, were less obvious about why I should have signed up to them as it was unclear where they would lead. It is valid to make some of these choices based on instinct, interest, or alignment with your core values, even if the final outcome is less obvious at the beginning.

Embed reflection as part of your everyday practice

Time moves fast, and once you are in a job with increasing levels of responsibility and deadlines, it can be easy to get caught up in the speed of everyday life and forget the lessons your PhD taught you about the importance of taking a moment to think before you leap into things. Be aware of how easy it is to lose the good habits you've developed and take a practical approach to maintaining them, like putting in some diary time, so you still identify time to reflect and use the outcome of those reflections to improve your work.

Be aware that dissemination is no longer just to an academic crowd

The world where it was OK for academics to just speak to academics about their work no longer exists. Even if you stay within academia, you will need to speak to a broad audience about what you are doing and why it matters. It is so important for us to get out of our buildings and libraries and go into communities to be able to talk about what we do and why it is brilliant. How will others know about what it is we do if we don't communicate about it? How can someone aspire to this career if they don't know it exists? Think of all the barriers you have overcome, and how much people sharing knowledge has helped you. When you are the holder of that knowledge, the onus is now on you to pass it on to help others overcome their challenges. You can't be what you can't see, so be visible.

Take every opportunity to practice your communication skills

Communication is a thread that will weave through everything you do, and spending time to become better at all aspects of it will reap benefits. Whether that is linked to having difficult conversations, pitching the level of detail needed by different audiences, or improving your ability to summarise information in limited word count.

Developing these skills for one context will also help when those skills are used in a different context. The requirement to communicate in so many different ways in academia is actually a real privilege and ideally should bring you enjoyment. If you don't find joy in it, it is worth exploring whether it is linked to a lack of confidence and addressing that early. Don't let a lack of confidence stop you developing, you are better than you think.

Be deliberate with your public and social media presence

The world has changed a lot from when I started training, but one of the main ways that it is different is the importance of engaging with social media and having a web presence in order to be successful. This form of presence isn't the same as your personal presence, where you might bemoan bad days at work with your friends and family. It is therefore worth deliberately separating these aspects of your life, so that you have areas where you disseminate your work and host a professional presence, and safe private spaces where you can chat with friends and family. In your professional spaces, always be professional, don't get drawn in to conversations and arguments that you wouldn't participate in if you weren't face to face. Rise above the drama and show your best self.

Actively support those who are following behind you

Remember the reason you bought this book? The reason you needed to search out more information in order to help you. There will be someone else in that same position, someone else who needs that help. You are now in a position to be the one that helps them. If you get the chance, be the person who steps up to help others, and then remind them to do the same.

Remember: this is only the beginning

A PhD can feel, and is often discussed like, it is the final step. In reality, finishing your PhD is just the glorious beginning. You have so much good stuff yet to come. Remember those lessons about celebration, and everything else you've learnt. You have a wonderful future ahead of you.

ABOUT THE AUTHOR

Professor Elaine Cloutman-Green is a Consultant Clinical Scientist working within Infection Prevention and Control and as Lead Healthcare Scientist for a world renowned paediatric hospital. She holds an Honorary Professorship with UCL and was awarded the British Empire Medal as part of the New Years Honours in 2021 for services to healthcare.

She started her Clinical Scientist training in 2004 in Microbiology and, during her training, she completed an MSc in Clinical Microbiology. In 2007, after completing her training, she specialised in Infection Prevention and Control. As part of this work she has undertaken a PhD whilst on the NIHR CSO Doctoral Fellowship scheme on 'The role of the environment in transmission of healthcare associated infection'. Her research on prevention of healthcare associated infection also includes the development and implementation of rapid typing schemes in order to identify transmission. In 2016 she was awarded an NIHR ICA Clinical Lectureship in order to continue this work.

In 2015 she successfully attained Fellowship of the Royal College of Pathologists and was appointed the first UK based International Ambassador for the Society of Healthcare Epidemiology of America. In 2016 she became a Fellow of the Higher Education Academy and was appointed as a NICE Expert Advisor in Infection Prevention and Control. She became a Consultant Clinical Scientist and Deputy Director of Infection Prevention and Control in 2021.

She is the Chair of the Environmental Network, a project she is especially passionate about as it is related to her PhD. She has held international roles as the UK Ambassador for the Society for Healthcare Epidemiology of America, and Country Ambassador for the American Society of Microbiology. She supports strategic and professional committee positions linked antimicrobial resistance, pedagogy, and Healthcare Science, as well as sitting on a number of national research committees. Follow @girlymicro on social media (all platforms) if you'd like to get in touch.

Printed in Dunstable, United Kingdom

78108933R00122